D1356774

The Prison Narratives
of Jeanne Guyon

AMERICAN ACADEMY OF RELIGION

AAR RELIGIONS IN TRANSLATION

SERIES EDITOR
Anne Monius, Harvard Divinity School

A Publication Series of
The American Academy of Religion
and
Oxford University Press

THE SABBATH JOURNAL OF JUDITH LOMAX
Edited by Laura Hobgood-Oster

THE ANTICHRIST LEGEND
A Chapter in Jewish and Christian Folklore
Wilhelm Bousset
Translated by A. H. Keane
Introduction by David Frankfurter

LANGUAGE, TRUTH, AND RELIGIOUS BELIEF
*Studies in Twentieth-Century Theory and Method in
Religion*
Edited by Nancy K. Frankenberry and Hans H. Penner

BETWEEN HEGEL AND KIERKEGAARD
Hans L. Martensen's Philosophy of Religion
Translations by Curtis L. Thompson and David J. Kangas
Introduction by Curtis L. Thompson

EXPLAINING RELIGION
Criticism and Theory from Bodin to Freud
J. Samuel Preus

DIALECTIC
or, The Art of Doing Philosophy
A Study Edition of the 1811 Notes

Friedrich D. E. Schleiermacher
Translated with Introduction and Notes by Terence
N. Tice

RELIGION OF REASON
Out of the Sources of Judaism

Hermann Cohen
Translated, with an Introduction by Simon Kaplan
Introductory essays by Leo Strauss
Introductory essays for the second edition by Steven
S. Schwarzchild and Kenneth Seeskin

DURKHEIM ON RELIGION
Émile Durkheim
Edited by W. S. F. Pickering

ON THE *GLAUBENSLEHRE*
Two Letters to Dr. Lücke
Friedrich D. E. Schleiermacher
Translated by James Duke and Francis Fiorenza

HERMENEUTICS
The Handwritten Manuscripts
Friedrich D. E. Schleiermacher

Edited by Heina Kimmerle
Translated by James Duke and Jack Forstman

THE STUDY OF STOLEN LOVE
Translated by David C. Buck and K. Paramasivam

THE DAOIST MONASTIC MANUAL
A Translation of the *Fengdao Kejie*
Livia Kohn

SACRED AND PROFANE BEAUTY
The Holy in Art

Garardus van der Leeuw
Preface by Mircea Eliade
Translated by David E. Green
With a new introduction and bibliography by Diane
Apostolos-Cappadona

THE HISTORY OF THE BUDDHA'S RELIC
SHRINE
A Translation of the Sinhala Thūpavamsa
Stephen C. Berkwitz

DAMASCIUS' *PROBLEMS & SOLUTIONS
CONCERNING FIRST PRINCIPLES*
Translated with Introduction and Notes by
Sara Ahbel-Rappe

THE SECRET GARLAND
Āṇṭāḷ's Tiruppāvai and Nācciyār Tirumoḷi
Translated with Introduction and Commentary by
Archana Venkatesan

PRELUDE TO THE MODERNIST CRISIS
The "Firmin" Articles of Alfred Loisy
Edited, with an Introduction by C. J. T. Talar
Translated by Christine Thirlway

DEBATING THE DASAM GRANTH
Robin Rinehart

THE FADING LIGHT OF ADVAITA ĀCĀRYA
Three Hagiographies
Rebecca J. Manring

THE UBIQUITOUS ŚIVA
Somānanda's Śivadṛṣti and His Tantric Interlocutors
John Nemec

PLACE AND DIALECTIC
Two Essays by Nishida Kitarō
Translated by John W.M. Krummel and Shigenori
Nagatomo

THE PRISON NARRATIVES OF
JEANNE GUYON
Ronney Mourad and Dianne Guenin-Lelle

AAR
AMERICAN ACADEMY OF RELIGION

The Prison Narratives of Jeanne Guyon

RONNEY MOURAD

DIANNE GUENIN-LELLE

OXFORD
UNIVERSITY PRESS

OXFORD
UNIVERSITY PRESS

Oxford University Press, Inc., publishes works that further
Oxford University's objective of excellence
in research, scholarship, and education.

Oxford   New York
Auckland   Cape Town   Dar es Salaam   Hong Kong   Karachi
Kuala Lumpur   Madrid   Melbourne   Mexico City   Nairobi
New Delhi   Shanghai   Taipei   Toronto

With offices in
Argentina   Austria   Brazil   Chile   Czech Republic   France   Greece
Guatemala   Hungary   Italy   Japan   Poland   Portugal   Singapore
South Korea   Switzerland   Thailand   Turkey   Ukraine   Vietnam

Published by Oxford University Press, Inc.
198 Madison Avenue, New York, New York 10016

www.oup.com

Oxford is a registered trademark of Oxford University Press.

Library of Congress Cataloging-in-Publication Data
Guyon, Jeanne Marie Bouvier de La Motte, 1648–1717.
[Récits de captivité. English]
The prison narratives of Jeanne Guyon / [translated by] Ronney Mourad and Dianne Guenin-Lelle.
p.   cm.
Includes bibliographical references (p.   ) and index.
ISBN 978-0-19-984112-7 (hardcover : alk. paper)
1. Guyon, Jeanne Marie Bouvier de La Motte, 1648–1717.   2. Catholics—France—Biography.
I. Mourad, Ronney.   II. Guenin-Lelle, Dianne.   III. Title.
BX4705.G8A3 2012
282.092—dc22 [B]   2011013692

1 3 5 7 9 8 6 4 2

Printed in the United States of America
on acid-free paper

Preface

THE IDEA FOR this book emerged as we were working on a volume about Jeanne Guyon for Paulist Press's Classics of Western Spirituality series. In that volume we translated and discussed selections from Guyon's *Life* and several of her other most important spiritual works. Given the lack of spiritual instruction in the *Prison Narratives*, however, we decided that this text could not be included there. We nonetheless became convinced of its importance for understanding Guyon's life and work. Many readers have studied and enjoyed her autobiography without access to this captivating conclusion, which has never before been published in English translation. We seek here to provide that translation and to demonstrate the historical, literary, and theological value of Guyon's prison writings.

Many people contributed to our efforts. We would like particularly to thank Bernard McGinn for reviewing the translation and Clark Gilpin for offering helpful advice on the project. The book would not have been possible at all without the pioneering scholarship of Marie-Louise Gondal and Dominique Tronc. Both of the anonymous reviewers for Oxford University Press provided detailed and helpful suggestions for improving the manuscript. We appreciate their critical reading and feedback. We also appreciate Anne Monius's editorial work on the project and her willingness to consider it for inclusion in the AAR/OUP Religion in Translation series. We are grateful to Emmanuel Yewah for his suggestions regarding the translation. Thanks are also due to Albion College for funding the sabbaticals during which much of the work was completed.

Our colleagues in Religious Studies and in Modern Languages and Cultures participated in many water-cooler conversations about the project, and we appreciate their interest and support. These include Jocelyn McWhirter, Selva Raj, Mark Soileau, Nancy Weatherwax, Emmanuel Yewah, Perry Myers, Cathie Grimm, Julia Medina, Kalen Oswald, and Linda Clawson.

We would also like to thank our friends and families. Ron is grateful to his wife, Emily Kuo, and his sons, Peter and Luke, for their love and support. At various times, Walid, Najat, Nawal, Greg, and Diana Mourad made the mistake of asking what he was working on and got an earful. Thanks are due for their patient listening and feedback. Dianne gives heartfelt thanks to her husband, Mark Lelle, for his love, support, and wonderful cooking, which sustained her body and spirit, as well as to her children, Hannah and Austin, for their love, patience, and growing interest in their mom's work. She would also like to thank Selma Zebouni, for introducing her to the complexities of seventeenth-century literature and cultural production, and Friends General Conference, for connecting her to Jeanne Guyon's work through that unassuming little book, *A Guide to True Peace*.

Contents

The Prison Narratives
of Jeanne Guyon

Introduction

THE FRENCH CATHOLIC mystic Jeanne Guyon (1648–1717) was imprisoned for over seven years on various charges related to her spiritual teaching
and writing. In the years following her release from prison, her works attracted
a large international readership, especially among Quakers and Pietists. Her
imprisonment was one of the most important reasons for her early influence
outside France, as many of her Protestant readers identified with her politically enforced marginalization and perceived her as a martyr.[1] Until recently,
however, relatively little had been published concerning Guyon's life in prison.
In her well-known autobiography, she reveals almost nothing about the physical conditions of her confinement after 1695, focusing instead—and only
briefly—on her spiritual state during these years. Her public silence concerning this period allowed her enemies to control French popular perceptions of
the Quietist Affair, the religious and political conflict initiated by her writings. The version of her *Life* published posthumously in 1720 has proven not
to be her last word on the subject, however. In 1709 she wrote an additional,
private conclusion to her autobiography for some of her close friends. This
text remained hidden for centuries until the discovery of an archival copy
made its publication possible in 1992. Guyon's early reputation among Protestants outside France was shaped by this gripping account of her confinement,
which her supporters copied and circulated. The text reveals the real religious
and political forces behind the Quietist Affair, and it vividly presents the
challenges Guyon faced as a female prisoner of conscience. It also clarifies the
literary strategy and theological purpose of Guyon's *Life* and illustrates both
the power and limits of Christian prison literature. These *Prison Narratives*
are translated into English for the first time here.

Some of the most powerful political and religious figures in seventeenth-
century France, including Louis XIV himself, conspired to bring about
Guyon's lengthy imprisonment. By isolating her from her friends and con-
trolling her daily life, Guyon's enemies were able to engineer her public disgrace and thereby discredit her mystical teachings in France. Guyon's *Prison*

Narratives testify to this process and present Guyon's spiritually motivated form of resistance to it. Her testimony possesses a stark, naked quality in its unadorned representation of her life as a political and religious captive. It also tells a story of unfailing faith—even at the most desperate moments. Throughout her imprisonment, Guyon remains true to her beliefs and maintains her complete submission to what she believes is the will of God, even at moments that could have, indeed should have, broken her spirit. She does not collapse under the weight of ongoing, coercive interrogations or yield to the physical and psychological wounds inflicted on her through acts of injustice, abuse, and calumny. Her narratives accordingly offer unique perspectives on several perennial theological issues: the meaning of evil and suffering, the balance of activity and passivity in the spiritual life, and the means of the soul's progress toward union with God.

The recent discovery of Guyon's *Prison Narratives* makes possible a reinterpretation of her historical, literary, and theological legacies. She is a controversial figure in many ways. The analysis below begins with a biographical sketch focusing on her formative intellectual influences and on the events that resulted in her imprisonment. Next we examine the history of the *Prison Narratives* and their relation to the published version of Guyon's *Life*. In the final section of the introduction we offer a close, interdisciplinary reading of Guyon's text drawing from cultural history, theology, literary studies, and women's studies. The text of the *Prison Narratives* has been translated in its entirety from Dominique Tronc's critical edition of Guyon's *Life*.[2]

Biographical Sketch

Jeanne-Marie Bouvier de la Mothe was born on April 13, 1648 in Montargis, a large French town about 70 miles south of Paris. Much of what scholars know about her youth is drawn from her long, detailed autobiography. According to this account, she was born prematurely and her family feared for several weeks that she would not survive. Both her mother and father had been in previous marriages that produced children. Jeanne-Marie was her father's favorite and, perhaps consequently, suffered neglect from her mother. From the age of two and a half, she was sent to live in convents that offered girls' boarding schools. Her experiences in these schools were mostly unfulfilling, both educationally and emotionally, although she was nurtured and challenged for a time in an Ursuline convent under the loving care of her older sister. Her parents moved her frequently between home and school as a child, probably as a result of their conflicting attitudes toward her. Her father preferred to have her at home, partly for fear that she would seek a monastic vocation against his wishes. Her mother, who showed little interest in her, spending her time instead on religious devotions and service to the Catholic Church, seems to have favored her brother and to have tacitly permitted his frequent cruelties toward her. Her father was often absent from the household and therefore did not witness much of his daughter's suffering. As a young adolescent, Jeanne-Marie was sickly and introspective. She desired a more comprehensive religious education than she received, but she was exposed to some popular spiritual works, such as the *Introduction to the Devout Life* by Francis de Sales and the *Life of St. Jane Frances de Chantal,* which deeply influenced her. These writings continued to be important to her throughout her life.

The prestige and nobility of the La Mothe family name made her marriage prospects very favorable. When she blossomed into a beautiful young woman in her early teens her mother took a newfound interest in her daughter and the attention she garnered in the Court of Louis XIV. However, any pleasure that this situation might have brought her was short-lived; in 1664, when she was fifteen, her parents arranged for her to marry a man she had never met, Jacques Guyon du Chesnoy, who was twenty-two years her senior and already the father of several children. Jeanne-Marie's marriage was presumably arranged out of financial interest, since the Guyon family was extremely wealthy. The marriage was not a happy one for many reasons, the most obvious being the couple's difference in age, but also the different backgrounds of the La Mothe family and the Guyon family. In her *Life* she explains how this situation was exacerbated by the presence of her mother-in-law, who sought to control all of her social interactions, religious observances, and household responsibilities, making life very difficult for her even after the death of her husband. Nevertheless, this union produced five children, three of whom grew to adulthood.

Early in her marriage, Guyon took to exploring prayer and mystical theology in ways that were unusual for a layperson, and all the more so for a young wife and mother. This new chapter in her life began to unfold when she met the Duchess of Charost, daughter of the disgraced former Minister of Finance, Nicolas Fouquet. Charost had sought refuge in the household of the La Mothe family when she was exiled from Court. Guyon was fascinated by Charost, and particularly by the forms of spiritual devotion she practiced. Through Charost, Guyon encountered the theology of Jacques Bertot, who had been influenced, in turn, by Jean de Bernières, a prominent mystic of the French School. Guyon became increasingly involved with a small circle of mystically inclined nobility. An important milestone along this path was her encounter with the Franciscan monk Archange

Enguerrand, who instructed her in the practice of contemplative prayer and introduced her to Geneviève Granger, the Mother Superior of the local Benedictine convent. She reports in her *Life* that her new interior awareness of God motivated her to cultivate several corresponding ascetic disciplines, including forms of corporal mortification.

Christians in seventeenth-century France pursued spiritual development in many different ways, and those differences were controversial. Guyon gravitated toward mystical forms of theology and prayer. The French term '*oraison*' (translated here as 'contemplative prayer') serves as a kind of shorthand reference in her writing to the tradition of "apophatic" or "negative" mystical devotion, in which the mystic seeks to turn her attention to God's presence in the soul without the mediation of language, rational thought, images, or individual desires. As Guyon's theology developed, she came to think that the soul in contemplative prayer invites God to erase its self-awareness and thereby enable a complete union with the divine. Within the mystical tradition there were competing understandings of how to achieve or even to articulate this goal. However, the mystics who engaged in this debate recognized that all their attempts at speaking about God necessarily fell short of the inarticulate awareness they sought. Their dialogue focused, therefore, on the usefulness and evocative power of terms and metaphors, rather than their correspondence to transcendent reality. By the seventeenth century, French advocates of this tradition had come to see it as a coherent and orthodox "science of the Saints," which they called *la mystique*.[3] Its foundational texts included the works of pseudo-Dionysius; the great German and Flemish mystics of the fourteenth and fifteenth centuries, such as Henry Suso, Johannes Tauler, Jan van Ruusbroec and Hendrik Herp; and the Spanish and Italian mystics of the sixteenth century, such as Teresa of Ávila, John of the Cross, and Catherine of Genoa. Guyon became familiar with all of these authors, and she also began to read the works of French mystics who had further developed this tradition in the seventeenth century.

In 1671, Guyon was introduced to the person who would play a pivotal role, first, in her spiritual development and, later, in absentia, in her long persecution—the Barnabite Friar François La Combe. Guyon's half-brother, Dominique La Mothe, introduced her to La Combe. At about the same time Mother Granger introduced her to Bertot, who became a major intellectual influence on Guyon, mainly through their extensive correspondence. Guyon's long friendship with a Jansenist priest eventually caused Bertot to distance himself from her after having given her spiritual guidance and support for several years. La Combe would later take on this role of spiritual director, becoming Guyon's closest friend and confidant in the years prior to her imprisonment.

Guyon's husband died in 1676 after twelve years of marriage. During his last days, he expressed remorse for his failures in their unhappy marriage and took steps to insure her financial security after his death. In spite of her freedom as an independent widow, she experienced several years of spiritual dryness until 1680, when she had another spiritual conversion. This conversion was accompanied by a sense of missionary purpose and a desire to travel to Geneva in order to convert Protestants to Catholicism. In particular, she hoped to work with the New Catholics, a religious community devoted to this project. She made the difficult decision to leave her home and family, after giving her brother-in-law control of her financial affairs and putting her mother-in-law in charge of her older children. Only her youngest daughter accompanied her on the trip. In her *Life* she speaks about the complete and unexpected transformation that occurred at this time in her relationship with her mother-in-law, which became loving and forgiving.

La Combe joined her at various points during her travels to Corbeil, Annecy, Gex, and Thonon. Guyon found this gentle priest to be a model of spirituality, honesty, and simplicity. For his part, La Combe found in Guyon a brilliant woman who had read widely in the mystical tradition and offered him compelling insights concerning prayer and personal sanctification. It was a friendship that sustained both of them for many years. However, this period in her relationship with La Combe would fuel many of the future calumnies directed against her. In the eyes of their enemies there was always a cloud of impropriety and sexual immorality surrounding their travels together, resulting principally from her status as a wealthy young widow eschewing the conventional gender norms that restricted "honorable" women to the control of family or convent. None of the rumors were ever proven, but with Guyon isolated and silenced in prison, their mere plausibility would suffice to discredit her. Indeed, her brother, who had introduced her to La Combe, openly criticized his sister's behavior (after he failed to acquire as much of her fortune as he coveted). In spite of Guyon's unconventional behavior, Jean d'Arenthon d'Alex, the Bishop of Geneva, still supported her at this time. She speculates in her *Life* that he also hoped to gain control of her income. D'Arenthon even made La Combe her official spiritual director. From Thonon, her family called her back to Paris. She returned there, never having reached Geneva.

Shortly thereafter, in 1682, she travelled back to the Ursuline convent in Thonon, where her understanding of her calling began to change. She increasingly saw herself as a teacher and author dedicated to deepening the spiritual lives of complacent Christians, rather than a missionary pursuing converts. She renounced much of her wealth and wrote the *Spiritual Torrents*, the first of many books to come. She also wrote the first edition of her *Life*. D'Arenthon pressured her to become prioress of the New Catholics in Gex, which would have assured him control over her remaining fortune—still a considerable sum. Guyon's attitude toward the New Catholics had changed, though, and she had come to disapprove of their coercive missionary tactics. She refused the position. It was this decision that marked the beginning of d'Arenthon's campaign against her, as he began to spread unfavorable reports about her mystical teachings and her relationship with La Combe. As a result of this rift, several powerful church leaders began to criticize her actions and monitor her activities. These troubles, which continued for over twenty years, did not deter Guyon from her apostolic mission, though d'Arenthon remained her nemesis until his death in 1695.

Guyon left Thonon to pursue her calling in the Savoy region of France and the Piedmont region of Italy. She established a hospital and continued her lifelong work of helping the poor. In Grenoble, she wrote her *Short and Easy Method of Prayer*, which was published in 1685, and her extensive, multi-volume *Explanation of the Holy Scripture*. One part of the latter work, her well-known *Commentary on the Song of Songs*, was published without her other commentaries in 1688. Not surprisingly, Guyon gained attention, much of it negative, for her remarkable actions. The fact that she, as a laywoman, was offering spiritual teaching, healing the sick, exorcizing the possessed, and writing on mystical subjects put her on a collision course with the most powerful clerics in France. The Bishop in Grenoble finally asked her to leave his diocese. After a brief stay in Turin she was asked to leave that city too. In 1686, after being denied permission to go to Geneva, she settled in Paris.

Guyon's return to Paris coincided with the trial of the Spanish priest Miguel de Molinos in Rome on charges of heretical teaching. In 1687, Pope Innocent XI condemned Molinos's mystical claims in a bull entitled *Coelestis Pastor*. Molinos's position, as summarized by the propositions condemned in this bull, came to be known as Quietism. Although Guyon insists in her *Life* that she had not been acquainted with Molinos's thought before this period in Paris, her detractors found significant similarities between her work and his. Most importantly, both mystics emphasized the importance of passive submission to God's activity in the soul, especially in the highest stages of contemplation. The central Quietist idea—that the soul can be so completely purified of self-interest, self-awareness, and individual desires that it achieves an abiding union with God—had several controversial implications. If

spiritually advanced mystics could completely annihilate individual preferences in complete submission to the divine will, how could they desire their
own salvation? How could they offer petitionary prayers? Did passive submission to God's guidance preclude the active cultivation of virtue? Guyon
touches on many of these difficult issues in her *Short and Easy Method*, and
though her positions are carefully nuanced, some of her detractors interpreted
them to be inconsistent with the official teaching in *Coelestis Pastor*.

Contemplative prayer had many critics in the seventeenth century. Mainstream Catholic piety in Guyon's time was centered on the performance of
the sacraments and participation in the liturgy of the calendar cycle. Some
opponents of mysticism argued that the meaning and function of prayer was
essentially derived from its role in these rituals, and therefore that it should
consist exclusively of petitions to God and the saints, as well as expressions of
praise, love, thanksgiving, or contrition for one's sins. Advocates of this traditional Catholic view feared that contemplative prayer might substitute a purportedly direct, but actually self-deceptive, mystical experience in place of the
sacramental experience of the divine presence. These fears were particularly
trenchant because of the ongoing threat of Protestantism, which had already
challenged the primacy of the Catholic sacraments in Christian spiritual life.
Additional criticism of contemplative prayer came from advocates of meditation. 'Meditation,' in its technical seventeenth-century usage, and in sharp
contrast with 'contemplative prayer,' referred to the use of intellect, imagination, and moral intuition to reach an honest self-assessment and to cultivate
personal virtue. The most influential techniques of meditation in Guyon's
time derived from the *Spiritual Exercises* of Ignatius of Loyola, the founder of
the Society of Jesus. Guyon's preference for a simple and easily accessible form
of contemplative prayer—a "prayer of the heart and not the head"—evidences
the distance between the path of her *Short and Easy Method* and the use of
various mental faculties in the dominant Jesuit techniques of meditation.[4]
Last, the rise of the scientific method in the seventeenth century was produc-
ing an epistemological shift in the interpretation of human experience. One
consequence of this shift was the increasing inclination among intellectuals to
interpret mystical phenomena as the effects of madness or (in women) hysteria rather than as signs of divine grace.

Coelestis Pastor empowered Guyon's enemies, including the brother who
had not forgotten their earlier financial dispute, to question her orthodoxy.
At the same time rumors were circulating in Paris claiming that La Combe
was guilty of various acts of impropriety and had betrayed his clerical office.
Thus, the strategy of those who opposed her teachings was already in place.

Formal investigations of theological transgressions coupled with surreptitious insinuations of social transgressions became characteristic of the many subsequent episodes in her long persecution. In October of 1687, La Combe became the first victim of such an investigation, led by François de Harlay de Champvallon, the politically ambitious Archbishop of Paris. La Combe was found guilty on charges of Quietism, based mainly on the suspicion of impropriety and heresy rather than any proof. He spent the rest of his life in prison, eventually losing his sanity from confinement and abuse. He died in an asylum, but not before his mental breakdown allowed Guyon's persecutors to claim many years later that he had incriminated her in a letter that suggested a sexual relationship between them.

Emboldened by the rejection of Quietism in *Coelestis Pastor* and the judgment against La Combe, the Bishop of Geneva soon condemned Guyon's *Short and Easy Method* in a pastoral letter, and Harlay had Guyon confined in Paris at the convent of the Visitation Sainte Marie on charges of heresy. Harlay's motivations seem to have been entirely worldly. He hoped to pressure Guyon to arrange a marriage between her daughter and his nephew, and the charges of Quietism provided a convenient pretext for him to gain the leverage he needed. Guyon claims in her *Life* that she was promised freedom if she would consent to this marriage. She rejected the offer and therefore remained imprisoned in the convent for seven months. She was interrogated by Léonard Pirot, a theologian at the Sorbonne, and Louis-Antoine de Noailles, the Bishop of Châlons. Noailles would become the next Archbishop of Paris after Harlay's death and would play an important role in Guyon's later imprisonment. He is portrayed in a very unflattering light in the *Prison Narratives*. After reviewing her writings and discussing them with her, Pirot could find no theological grounds on which to condemn Guyon. While confined, Guyon returned to her autobiographical project, writing several new chapters about her life between 1682 and 1688.

When her good friend Madame de Miramion asked Madame de Maintenon, the uncrowned Queen of France, to intercede on Guyon's behalf, she appealed to the general acknowledgment at Court that the grounds for her imprisonment were baseless. Guyon was released, and Harlay burned all the official papers concerning the case. The episode cost him some of his good standing at Court. Louis XIV acknowledged in his order of release that the only evidence motivating Guyon's confinement was a false letter. Upon her release she was able to enjoy the company of her lifelong friends, many of whom were also influenced by Bertot. These included the Duke and Duchess of Chevreuse, the Duke and Duchess of Beauvillier and the Duchess of

Mortemart. The duchesses were daughters of Jean-Baptiste Colbert, Louis XIV's beloved Minister of Finance, and Madame de Chevreuse was perhaps the most favored woman at Court. As a follower of Bertot, Madame Charost was also very close to these three families, as was François de Salignac de la Mothe-Fénelon, a childhood friend of the Duke of Beauvillier. These friends had a reputation for piety and were particularly devoted to the practice of contemplative prayer and the study of mystical theology. Many of them also became Guyon's confidants and lifelong defenders.

Madame de Maintenon was drawn to this devout group and came to admire Guyon's writings. She claimed always to carry a copy of the *Short and Easy Method* and to have read it to Louis XIV. During this period Guyon would sometimes visit her first cousin, Marie-Françoise de La Maisonfort, who lived at St-Cyr, a school for girls near Versailles founded by Madame de Maintenon. Madame de Maisonfort asked Madame de Maintenon to engage Guyon as a spiritual advisor to these young noblewomen. In 1688 Guyon began her work there, which was to last several years. This appointment marked the pinnacle of Guyon's influence at Court. She earned the respect of many of the most powerful people in France, including her future enemy, Jacques-Bénigne Bossuet, the Bishop of Meaux. At this time, she and Fénelon also began an extensive correspondence on mystical topics. Fénelon was soon named the Preceptor of the Duke of Bourgogne, grandson of Louis XIV and second in line for the throne. This made Fénelon the second most important cleric in France, after Bossuet. He was well respected for his intellect, writings, and moral rectitude, and he was gaining ever greater influence at Court.

However, the tide at Court shifted politically and theologically in the early 1690s, and those associated with Quietism came under scrutiny once again—this time more than ever. The privileged status that Guyon, Fénelon, and their friends enjoyed, as evidenced by their close relationship to Madame de Maintenon, was a double-edged sword. If Guyon's ideas were discredited for any reason, it would no longer affect her alone. It would reflect badly on her patrons as well. In a political situation in which power and status depended heavily on the appearance of social rectitude and unimpeachable relationships, the controversial character of Guyon's mysticism became a possible liability for Madame de Maintenon and others. When Guyon's critics began to voice their objections again, she found herself abandoned and even attacked by many of her former allies who wished to distance themselves from her. Quite aware that there was growing suspicion of her practices among others at Court, Guyon was even convinced that she had been secretly poisoned.

Charges of improper behavior and insubordination at St-Cyr also fueled the criticism of Quietist teaching. Some of these incidents involved Guyon's cousin, Madame de Maisonfort, who was one of the most influential teachers at the school and was being groomed as its future director. Her indiscretions, as well as those of some of the students, were connected, rightly or wrongly, with Guyon's emphasis on passive submission to God's will. Critics of mystical theology had associated it with antinomian behavior for centuries, but Quietism was particularly exposed to this charge because of its emphasis on the passivity of the individual's will. If the mystic's own will was completely united with God's will, critics claimed, then the mystic might excuse apparently immoral behavior as an instance of special divine guidance. The problems at St-Cyr were seen as proof of the danger inherent in Guyon's teachings. Not surprisingly, the advocacy of contemplative prayer and other practices suspected of Quietist influence became a liability for the school and for Madame de Maintenon, who turned against Guyon. In 1693 Madame de Maintenon asked Guyon not to return to St-Cyr after the Bishop of Chartres objected to her writings and to Madame de Maisonfort's behavior.

After Madame de Maintenon dismissed her from her position at Saint-Cyr, Guyon understood that she needed theological allies to resist the powerful political and religious forces organizing against her. She solicited Bossuet's help, even sharing her unpublished autobiography with him. He read this text along with her published works in 1693, and, though he apparently did not initially consider her views heretical, he did form an unfavorable opinion of her. He particularly objected to what he considered exaggerated and prideful claims in her *Life* concerning her own advancement in the mystical life and her ability to serve as a vehicle of divine grace through a form of supernatural spiritual communication between souls. It did not help matters that Bossuet had had little exposure to the Catholic mystical tradition and therefore found many of Guyon's mystical claims more peculiar, or radical, than they really were.

It is interesting to note that Bossuet and other critics—such as Louis-Antoine de Noailles, the Archbishop of Paris who features prominently in the *Prison Narratives*—objected both to excessive pride in Guyon's writings (especially in her autobiography) and to excessive passivity in her doctrine of complete submission to the divine will. Speaking of her interactions with Bossuet, for example, Guyon writes, "I learned further that one of the great complaints of M. de Meaux was that I would praise myself and was horribly presumptuous."[5] Such accusations of self-aggrandizement certainly seem, on the face of things, to be in tension with accusations of problematic self-abnegation. The problem, according to Bossuet, was Guyon's (prideful, on his view) claim that she had surrendered her will so thoroughly to God that she was no longer capable of performing acts based on her own desires (and hence embraced a passivity incompatible with petitionary prayer, the virtuous desire for her own salvation, and active effort on behalf of moral improvement).

Regarding the accusations of pride, Guyon answers that she aims only to document the unmerited spiritual gifts God has given her, even though she knows that doing so will subject her to ridicule and humiliation. She adds, "I would willingly ask who is more humble,...he who humbles himself or he who is very happy to be humiliated?"[6] Guyon addresses the objections to her doctrine of the will in several of her works. Essentially, she argues that although very advanced souls find themselves unable to act virtuously by the power of their wills alone (since their wills have been joined to the divine will in an act of complete submission), God supplies virtuous desires for them, in accord with divine purposes. In her *Life*, for example, she writes, "the perceived desire, being an act and an operation of the self, must die with the other acts or, rather, must pass into God in order no longer to have desires other than those that God gives.... This does not prevent God from causing one to desire and to will to do what pleases him, and he who makes the soul can move it to desire, although it no longer has desires of its own."[7] Even if Bossuet could have acknowledged that such a complete submission to the divine will is possible or advisable in this life—and he was far from doing so—he certainly did not think Guyon had achieved it: "M. de Meaux claimed that there were only four or five people in the world who had these ways of praying and who would have difficulty performing acts."[8] Thus, the discussions between Guyon and Bossuet failed to provide the protection she sought and even put her in greater peril.

Madame de Maintenon became firmly determined to discredit Guyon. Rumors of her imminent imprisonment began to spread. To help stave off this threat, with the help of her influential friends, she requested a theological examination of her work. As a result, the Issy Conferences, a formal doctrinal inquiry into her writing, began in 1694. Her examiners included Bossuet, Noailles, and Louis Tronson, the Superior of Saint-Sulpice. Starting in February of 1695, Fénelon joined in the deliberations. He served both as a judge of Guyon's orthodoxy and also as an expert in the history of Catholic mystical theology. During the examination, Guyon consented to confinement in Bossuet's diocese of Meaux at the convent of Saint Marie. Bossuet kept her there for interrogation until March of 1695, when the *Articles of Issy* were published.

Rather than condemning particular heretical claims, the *Articles of Issy* presented its findings affirmatively, issuing thirty-four orthodox pronouncements concerning spiritual life, contemplative prayer, and mysticism. This document was signed by the examiners, including Fénelon, and Guyon submitted to its findings as well. She refused to sign an attestation of heresy, however, despite new demands from Bossuet that she do so. She insisted that her works were consistent with the *Articles* when properly interpreted. Under pressure from Madame de Maintenon, Bossuet disagreed and condemned her *Short and Easy Method* in a pastoral letter. The Issy Conferences did not give Bossuet all he had wished. Guyon's faith and her actions were not explicitly condemned, and her friends at Court still considered her a saint. Bossuet let her leave Meaux, but later, influenced by Madame de Maintenon, he tried again to secure an admission of heresy from her. She refused, this time by letter. Upon her release from Meaux, Guyon went into hiding. Bossuet and Madame de Maintenon were now acting in concert against her, with the former pursuing Guyon over issues of religious doctrine and the latter challenging her moral and social propriety. Although Guyon was in imminent peril, her friends did not lose their privileged positions at Court.

During this period Fénelon, in particular, did what few people at Court dared to do; he openly criticized Louis XIV. In his roles as confidant of Madame de Maintenon, preceptor of the Duke of Bourgogne, and esteemed public theologian, his writings had a powerful influence. In his ongoing correspondence, Fénelon boldly criticized the King in ways that were extraordinary for this time. The first such criticism, written between 1692 and 1693, is found in his "Lettre au roi Louis XIV." In this letter Fénelon criticizes the King for conducting unjust wars, for ruining France and for following advisors who had steered him away from the path of biblical truth and justice.[9] He encourages the King to change his policies and practices, and perhaps even his advisors. This letter was apparently in Madame de Maintenon's possession for over two years. Biographers claim that upon reading the letter Louis XIV became so infuriated that he decided to have Guyon imprisoned at Vincennes immediately. He needed to be more patient with Fénelon and, for the moment, simply kept a close watch on him.[10] Guyon was an easier target than Fénelon. She had exposed herself by writing on subjects that were not acceptable for a female author at the time and by teaching publicly. She was not protected by ties to a religious order. The King's decision would appear to be justified by Bossuet's recent condemnation of her writings, so there would be less suspicion about the political motivation for her incarceration. Thus, Guyon became a pawn in two larger struggles: a political one between

Fénelon and the King and, later, a theological one between Fénelon and Bossuet. The first struggle was the initial cause of Guyon's imprisonment, but the second one perpetuated it, as the public theological debate about Quietism continued for years. Fénelon became Guyon's apologist when she was not allowed to speak.

On December 21, 1695 Madame de Maintenon gave Noailles, the newly invested Archbishop of Paris, Fénelon's "Lettre au roi Louis XIV." She argued that it was impermissibly critical of and discouraging to the King, and Noailles agreed that the letter was too strident.[11] Guyon's *Prison Narratives* begin at this point. She was taken into custody on December 27, 1695, six days after Noailles received a copy of Fénelon's letter, and sent to Vincennes, where she remained for nearly two years. She was the only prisoner ever to be confined in this dungeon under a false name.[12]

Guyon writes in the *Prison Narratives* that she continued to undergo interrogations, much as she had in Meaux, but they became more aggressive and increasingly focused on her personal life instead of her theology. At this point, for the public, the Quietist controversy in France still centered primarily on Guyon, while Fénelon still appeared to enjoy the King's favor. For courtiers, however, there was an indication earlier in 1695 that Fénelon's place was less assured than perhaps it appeared when he was made Archbishop of Cambrai—an appointment that had little prestige. Many had expected him to be Harlay's successor.[13] Fénelon and Guyon's other friends tried to obtain her release, but they met a wall of resistance.

Guyon's situation changed for the worse when she was moved to a very small, dilapidated convent house in Vaugirard for the second stage of her imprisonment, which lasted over nineteen months. She was monitored there by a few nuns and a parish priest from Saint-Sulpice in Paris, Joachim Trotti de La Chétardie. She suffered constant harassment, manipulation, and mistreatment from these keepers. Since she had been the victim of nearly a decade of calumny, it is not surprising that the women living with her believed her to be dangerous and wicked, a person to be feared. They used her reputation to justify stealing from her, assaulting her, and, as she claims in her *Prison Narratives*, even trying to kill her.

Although Guyon's interrogators expressed little interest in her mysticism, the debate between Fénelon and Bossuet about Quietism became increasingly public. In February of 1697 Fénelon published his *Explanations of the Maxims of the Saints on the Interior Life*, which attempted to show that many of Guyon's ideas had precedents in the Catholic mystical tradition and had long been associated with officially acceptable, and even saintly, contemplative practices.[14] In addition, acting as Guyon's spokesman, he proposed a reading of the *Articles of Issy* that was favorable to Guyon's position, as well as his own. Bossuet published his *Instruction on the States of Prayer* one month later, condemning apophatic and passive types of prayer and defending the active use of the imagination, intellect, and will in pursuit of spiritual development. He argued that union with God was possible, but that in all of Christian history, only a few of the great contemplative saints had achieved it. Unlike Guyon, who had claimed that "Everyone is capable of inward contemplative prayer,"[15] Bossuet contended that divine union depended entirely on rare, supernatural acts of grace. When theological arguments failed to resolve the conflict, Bossuet turned to polemic. His *Account of Quietism*, published the following year, attacked Guyon and Fénelon personally. Bossuet drew from details in Guyon's *Life* to portray her as a mad visionary who had beguiled Fénelon with her religious delusions. This book's sensationalism had high entertainment value not only in Paris, but also in Rome. Bossuet's position won public favor.

Fénelon occupied an ever more vulnerable position. His *Maxims of the Saints* was a powerful, original defense of the apophatic tradition in Catholicism, but it was too dry and scholarly to sway the reading public. Although Fénelon had received official permission to publish the book, after his public disputes with Bossuet he decided to submit it for judgment in Rome. Guyon's fate came to depend on the vicissitudes of Fénelon's trial, as his enemies sought to affect the outcome by tarnishing her reputation. Fénelon had the support of Pope Innocent XII, but Louis XIV exerted strong political pressure to bias the proceedings against him. When Fénelon requested in June 1697 to go to Rome during the deliberations, not only did Louis XIV deny the request, but he banished him from court and ordered him to stay in Cambrai, where he was later stripped of his title as Preceptor of the Duke de Bourgogne. Finally, in 1699, Innocent XII issued a papal brief entitled *Cum Alias* that mildly condemned twenty-three propositions taken from Fénelon's *Maxims of the Saints*. Although technically a victory, this outcome was a blow to Bossuet and Louis XIV, who thought that they could compel the Pope to rule against Fénelon much more forcefully and to declare his book heretical. Fénelon's submission to the brief allowed him to preserve his office and improve his public status.

In addition to advocating mystical theology and defending Guyon's writings, Fénelon continued to develop his criticisms of Louis XIV's government. His most famous text on the subject, one that is still part of the French literary canon, is *Telemachus*. This novel criticizing the monarchy for its abuse of power was written as a guide for the Duke de Bourgogne on enlightened and just leadership. It was circulated at Court in 1698 before being published in 1699. Its position on just governance was a major influence on political theory in France in the eighteenth century and ultimately contributed to the French Revolution of 1789. The King was so outraged by the premise of *Telemachus* that, in retaliation against Fénelon, who had already been banished from Court,[16] he had Guyon transferred to the Bastille on June 4, 1698.

In the play of appearances and reality, there had to be a public pretext for transferring Guyon to the Bastille. It was time once again to resuscitate the charge of improper conduct between Guyon and La Combe. A new letter attributed to La Combe emerged, dated January 9, 1698, in which he expresses regret for his excesses and lapses in his relationship with Guyon. Guyon insists in the *Prison Narratives* that this letter was forged. If it were legitimate, it would have been written after La Combe had been imprisoned for eleven years and had become psychologically unstable. In order to discredit the authenticity of the letter, Guyon asked to confront her "accuser" directly. Although her captors gave public indications of arranging a meeting between the two, La Combe was committed to an insane asylum in Charenton before the meeting could take place—a fact that Bossuet worked to keep concealed.

At the Bastille, Guyon's situation deteriorated further. Although Fénelon's case was resolved in 1699, Guyon remained in prison without facing any formal charges. The harsh interrogations and the abuse by servants and others charged with caring for her continued, as her requests to be given a trial by the Parliament were consistently denied. After Fénelon's trial was over, Guyon's imprisonment no longer served much political purpose. In 1700 the Assembly of the Clergy, presided over by Bossuet, issued a statement finding her innocent of heretical intentions or moral turpitude.[17] There was, nonetheless, no sign of her imminent release. In the absence of a plausible explanation for her continued imprisonment, she speculates in the *Prison Narratives* that to release her would have harmed the reputation of her opponents by making her extraordinary persecution seem arbitrary. It would not be easy for them to change their minds, she writes, "when things have been pushed to certain extremes."[18] Meanwhile, she and the Quietist Affair were slipping from the public's attention.

One consideration that contributed to her eventual release, and influenced the conditions of her imprisonment, was that of her nobility and wealth. Although Guyon could not count on much help from her family, she still had influential friends, and the King's power did depend on support from the nobility. It is possible that gradual pressure from her supporters overcame

worries about the appearance of unfairness in her case and hastened her release. The effects of Guyon's social class on her physical circumstances in
prison are evident throughout her *Prison Narratives*. Her case was typical in
this respect: "prisoners were treated differently according to class and court
rank, reflecting the Old Regime's dislike of uniform laws... Prisoners paid en-
trance and exit fees as well as all jailing costs, and money could buy anything,
including a private cell, or *pistol*, food from outside, a mattress, music, and
heat."[19] Although Guyon's wealth did not diminish the cruelty of her captors
or the pain caused by her public disgrace, it did allow her to live comfortably
and to keep two servants with her in Vincennes and in Vaugirard. Her income
was used to buy books, food, and wine during her confinement, and she never
complains of hunger in her narrative. In the Bastille, she was allowed to use
her own resources to furnish her cell, and she did not have to share it with
another prisoner.

Guyon's imprisonment finally ended in 1703. Some of her persecutors,
such as Noailles, showed signs of remorse for the roles they had played in
her case, especially given her age and infirmity. The King sent word that
her children would be able to see her. This was the first step toward her
liberation. Sadly, this reunion with her children was not a pleasant turn of
events for Guyon, who was not only a liability, but also virtually a stranger
to them. Nonetheless, Guyon was released from the Bastille on March 24,
1703 into the care of her eldest son Jacques, who accepted legal responsibility for his mother. In a terse paragraph, Guyon summarizes her life in his
household: "You alone know, O my God, the nature of the sufferings of all
sorts that I endured in the course of the three or four years that I lived
there."[20]

Upon Bossuet's death in 1704, Guyon enjoyed more freedom to pursue
her calling as a spiritual guide and author. A collection of her writings was
published in the Netherlands that same year. She eventually received permission to live apart from her son, and the Bishop of Blois helped her find acceptable living arrangements for the next several years. The last twelve years of her
life were very full, as many of her readers—mostly Protestants from outside of
France—began to seek out her spiritual advice. She turned to writing poetry,
letters of spiritual direction, and, in 1709, the *Prison Narratives* and the final
edition of her *Life*. She remained in contact with some of her friends at Court
and with Fénelon until his death in 1715. However, in the last years of her life
she increasingly turned her attention toward the international and ecumenical group of followers who would disseminate her ideas in both Europe and
America. She died of natural causes in 1717.

The History of the Prison Narratives *and Their Relation to Guyon's Other Writings*

The Provenance and Authenticity of the Manuscript

The text translated here was discovered by Marie-Louise Gondal, with the help of archivists, in the late 1980s.[21] She had it published for the first time in French in 1992 under the title *Récits de captivité, Inédit: Autobiographie, Quatrième partie*. Though conserved for a time in the Jesuit Bibliothèque des Fontaines, its prior archival history and ownership are largely unknown. The physical, handwritten manuscript provides no clues about these matters: "it presents itself as a part of the autobiography of Mme Guyon. But it bears on itself neither title, nor signature, nor material signs of authentication. A different writer, more recent than that of the manuscript itself has, moreover, added the vague title, 'Account of Mme. Guyon.'"[22] The handwriting is not Guyon's or that of any of her known friends at the time of its composition in 1709. Several names are misspelled in the text. Gondal concludes from this evidence that the manuscript has been copied from another, and may even be "a copy of a copy."[23] No other copies of the text are presently known to exist.

The narrative is written from Guyon's perspective and picks up her story where her published autobiography ends. Guyon wrote her *Life* in three different stages. She composed the first part in 1682 and returned to the project in 1688, then again in 1709, several years after her release from prison. The opening paragraph of the *Prison Narratives* indicates that the text is connected to the *Life*. Guyon writes there that she did not intend to publish it but rather to share it with a small group of her friends, and she alludes to several reasons articulated in the *Life* for this decision. It therefore seems that in 1709 Guyon wrote the story of her imprisonment as the final part of her autobiography but had reservations about publishing it. She withheld the text and wrote a separate ending for the version of her *Life* meant for publication, in which she alludes only briefly and elliptically to the period after 1695. At some point after 1709, she sent this public version to Pierre Poiret, a fellow mystic living in the Netherlands, who had begun printing her other writings in 1704. Due perhaps to a conflict between Poiret and Andrew Michael Ramsey, a Scottish mystic who served as Guyon's secretary beginning in 1714, Guyon's *Life* was not published until 1720, after Poiret's death.[24] The published version did not include the *Prison Narratives*.

Despite the lack of a signature or recognizable handwriting (neither of which would be expected on a copy), the authenticity of the manuscript seems quite clear. Gondal argues for this point on the grounds of style and thematic content. She also points out that the *Prison Narratives* include several paragraphs identical to the closing sections of Part 3, Chapter 20 of the published version of Guyon's *Life*. These paragraphs describe events and dispositions belonging chronologically to the period of her imprisonment. This common material suggests that the two texts were originally part of a single autobiography. She may have borrowed a few paragraphs from the *Prison Narratives* to compose an ending for the *Life*. It is also possible that the borrowing went the other way, and she drew on material originally written for the *Life* to complement the *Prison Narratives* after separating the texts.

There is additional evidence of the text's authenticity. Guyon writes about the excessive interrogations she endured in the dungeon of Vincennes, which were conducted in 1696 by the Parisian Lieutenant General of Police, Gabriel Nicolas de La Reynie. Dominique Tronc has recently published the official records of these interrogations and demonstrated their coherence with Guyon's account in the *Prison Narratives*.[25] Furthermore, many other events included in the *Prison Narratives* are independently attested to in private letters Guyon wrote to her friend, the Duchess of Mortemart, during her confinement in Vaugirard. Tronc has also compiled excerpts from several of these letters supporting the authenticity of the *Prison Narratives*.[26] Among other topics, both sources discuss Guyon's conflicts with Joachim Trotti de La Chétardie, the parish priest who engineered her public disgrace, and an episode in which she was served poisoned wine.

The *Prison Narratives* and Guyon's Other Writings

The relation between the *Prison Narratives* and the public edition of Guyon's *Life* is interesting and a bit puzzling. Although the texts are similar in syntax, vocabulary, and theological perspective, they differ significantly in their content. The *Life* alternates between presentations of the major events in Guyon's life on the one hand and long, meditative digressions on the other. In these digressions she sometimes discusses her own spiritual states and sometimes offers didactic expositions of her views on mysticism and prayer. The *Prison Narratives*, in contrast, have very few of these sorts of digressions. For the most part, the text recounts the events comprising her life in prison and offers only brief self-descriptions to convey her responses. On rare occasions, such as the following, these descriptions are introspective: "It is necessary for me to talk about the disposition of my heart and all the sacrifices that God had me make in this house in Vaugirard. First, in spite of the storms there, I was in a state of very great tranquility, waiting from one moment to the next for the order of providence, to which I am devoted without reserve. My heart continually sacrificed without sacrifice, happy to be the victim of providence."[27] More often, though, when confronted with difficult circumstances, Guyon reports that God graced her with the patience to rely on the divine will and to trust in its ultimate benevolence. She emphasizes in several places that this spiritual gift—the theological virtue of patience—allows her to submit to her captors and to ignore provocations to anger, despite the fact that her "natural state was quick tempered."[28] For example, after the nun serving as her warden in Vaugirard insults and threatens her, she reports that "the One for whom I suffered gave me patience and did not permit me to let the least complaint escape. I did not speak to the parish priest about what had happened, and I abandoned everything to God."[29] Both of these types of self-presentation contrast strongly with the pages and pages of spiritual reflection common in the *Life*.

Nicholas Paige offers a compelling explanation of this change in Guyon's autobiographical writing. He argues that in 1682 and 1688, when Guyon wrote the early parts of her *Life*, she viewed the autobiographical genre as an appropriate medium for communicating her understanding of prayer and spiritual growth. Guyon believed that, after years of prayer followed by a period of spiritual dryness and then one of increasingly profound union with God, she had ascended to what she called the "apostolic state." Her first mention of this state in the *Life* occurs at the end of Part 2, Chapter 8, where she describes her calling to teach, despite having declined a traditional monastic appointment with the New Catholics in Gex. She wrote her first major work, the *Spiritual Torrents*, shortly thereafter, in 1682. Souls in the apostolic state are called, like Christ, to teach others and to suffer as a result: "when it pleased God to want to honor me with his mission, he made me understand that the true father in Jesus Christ, and the apostolic pastor, must suffer like him for men, bear their lethargy, pay their debts, be dressed in their weaknesses."[30] Guyon claims that her particular mission was not the conversion of Protestants in Geneva, as she had initially thought. She writes, "He made me understand that he was not calling me, as I first believed, to a propagation of the exterior of the Church, which consists of winning over heretics, but to the propagation of his Spirit, which is only ever the interior spirit, and that it would be for this Spirit that I would suffer. He does not destine me even for the first conversion of sinners, but for those who are touched by the desire to convert themselves in the perfect conversion."[31] Guyon wrote the first parts of her autobiography in pursuit of this apostolic mission. Her introspective spiritual digressions can therefore be understood as an attempt to cultivate in her readers the dispositions and forms of prayer conducive to spiritual growth as she understood it. She presents herself as a model of such dispositions, Paige argues, and she seems to have believed that the example of her inner life would inspire them more effectively than an abstract spiritual treatise ever could.[32]

Paige speculates that Guyon curtailed her spiritual reflections while writing in 1709 because she had lost confidence in the transparency and pedagogical efficacy of the autobiographical genre, and perhaps of prose in general. He argues that this loss of confidence resulted from Bossuet's uncharitable interpretation, and even mockery, of the early parts of the *Life*.[33] As discussed above, Bossuet was one of Guyon's examiners at the Conference of Issy in 1695. Although her *Life* was still incomplete at that point, Guyon hoped to strengthen her case at Issy by sharing it with Bossuet, who promised to treat it as a confession and to keep it private. He promptly betrayed her. She writes, "I had confided the story of my life to him, as I have already said, under the seal of confession. My most secret dispositions were written there. However, I learned that he had shown it to others and had made jokes about it."[34] Even worse, Bossuet used the *Life* to ridicule Guyon publicly in his *Account of Quietism*, published in 1698. In a famous passage, for example, Bossuet writes, "In the autobiography of the lady, I read that God bestowed upon her such an abundance of grace that she literally was bursting, and that her corset had to be unlaced."[35] Bossuet had demonstrated to Guyon that the spiritual introspection in her account could be interpreted as evidence of pride or madness rather than spiritual growth and sanctification. Perhaps, then, she had come to believe that the meaning of such introspective writing was opaque. If she no longer trusted her autobiographical writing to help bring about spiritual transformation in her readers, she may have written the final parts of her story in pursuit of other goals.

One consideration that undermines Paige's position is that Guyon wrote the *Prison Narratives* for a group of close friends whose views on mysticism she shared. She may therefore have intended the *Life*, but not the *Prison Narratives*, to serve as spiritual instruction simply because she wrote the two texts for different audiences—and not necessarily because she had lost faith in the transparency of the autobiographical genre during the Quietist Affair. Accordingly, she might have considered long, didactic digressions in the *Prison Narratives* unnecessary or even distracting. This consideration is not definitive, however. Paige's position still helps to explain the shift in Guyon's writing as a whole, including her increasing turn to poetry after her release from prison. And perhaps her unwillingness to write for a broader audience itself resulted from a loss of confidence in the spiritual value of prosaic instruction.

Although Paige's explanation for the difference in content between the *Life* and the *Prison Narratives* is therefore plausible, it is also possible to develop a complementary theological explanation for this difference. Guyon might have had relatively little to say about the state of her soul in the *Prison Narratives* because she was committed to the claim that this period of her life was spiritually consistent. In the meditation that concludes the public version of the *Life*, Guyon writes, "In these last times I am only able to speak about my dispositions a little bit or not at all, meaning that my state became simple and invariable. When I speak here of a fixed and permanent state, as in my other writings, I do not speak of an immutable state, which one cannot diminish. I call it permanent and fixed in relation to the states that have preceded it, which are full of vicissitudes and variations.... The base of this state is a profound annihilation, finding nothing nameable in me."[36] Like other apophatic mystics, Guyon claims here that the highest spiritual states are ineffable; they cannot be described in positive terms because awareness in these stages excludes the mediation of concepts or language. Such states are characterized by the soul's union with God, brought about by the complete loss of the self. Without personal desires or preferences, or even self-awareness, she argues, the mystic loses the ability to differentiate the self from the world or from God, and consciousness comes to consist of an undifferentiated sense of oneness.[37] Since Guyon claims to have entered into this state in the closing pages of her *Life*, it would be quite inconsistent for her to reflect at length on her purportedly ineffable state in the *Prison Narratives*. Furthermore, since the "interior" narration of the *Life* focuses principally on Guyon's spiritual advances and setbacks, it would not make sense for her to continue this narration in the *Prison Narratives*. She insists that the period of her life that was marked by such advances and setbacks has ended, and the condition of her soul has become "invariable."

The main theological task left to her in the *Prison Narratives* is to offer an interpretation of her incarceration that is consistent with these spiritual claims. She does so largely by accepting her ongoing suffering as a fitting means for adhering ever more closely to the state of the crucified Christ, a process that she expects to last a lifetime. In her closing sentence she writes, "I do not doubt that my dear Master will save up fiercer and stronger, though less dazzling, crosses for me, until the end of my days." This theme will be explored more fully below. Beyond this, as mentioned above, her brief self-descriptions focus very consistently on her equanimity in response to suffering

and her disinterestedness in her own fate. Such self-descriptions are exactly
what one would expect from someone claiming to have achieved union with
God through self-annihilation. Her emphasis on the theological virtue of patience also follows from these claims. If her will is united with the divine will,
the only "direct" action left to her is continual submission to God. All of her
other acts are "indirect," as she puts it in her *Short and Easy Method of Prayer*,
because once the soul submits fully to God, its subsequent acts depend on
God's initiative.[38] Such a soul could only resist the injustice of persecution if
God impelled it to do so. But God acts instead to preserve Guyon's state of
self-annihilation by means of her Christ-like suffering and therefore gives her
patience, rather than resistance, to achieve this end. Guyon summarizes these
implications of her theological position in her *Life*: "This made me understand that there was one kind of direct act without reflection, and I was acquainted with it through a continual exercise of love and faith, which,
rendering the soul submissive to all events of providence, becomes the door to
a veritable hatred of self, only loving crosses, ignominies, opprobrium."[39]

This theological explanation of Guyon's shift in the *Prison Narratives*
away from the detailed introspection characteristic of the *Life* may receive
some support from a brief stylistic consideration of her other best-known
works. The emphasis on self-abandonment and the spiritual value of suffering in the *Prison Narratives* is very consistent with these other works. She
was not writing this text to renounce her earlier mystical teaching or to in-
troduce new theological topics. Guyon presents Christian spiritual growth
as a lifelong process of transformation away from the self and toward union
with God. In many of her writings, such as the *Spiritual Torrents*, the *Short
and Easy Method of Prayer*, and her *Commentary on the Song of Songs*, she
discusses the most important steps in this process at length and ends with a
vision of its "consummation" through union with God. In each of these texts,
as in the *Life*, Guyon pays particularly close attention to the painful stages of
self-abandonment, as God intermittently lures the soul then leaves it to its
experiences of spiritual dryness and suffering. Her depiction of the process
of purification leading to self-abandonment is the most creative and detailed
aspect of her spiritual writings. Her descriptions of the state of permanent
union, in contrast, are shorter and less inventive. Analogously, the *Prison
Narratives* represents the consummation of the spiritual journey detailed in
Guyon's *Life*. Her shift away from lengthy psychological introspection in the
former is therefore true to form. As in her other works, her relative brevity
on the topic of mystical union seems, at least in part, to be a consequence of
the difficulty of discussing an inherently elusive subject.

Historical, Literary, and Theological Reflections

The Social Context of Guyon's Imprisonment

The length and severity of Guyon's imprisonment and the charges she faced raise difficult questions. Even Guyon's own presentation of these matters in the *Prison Narratives* may seem strange to contemporary readers. Guyon argues in many passages that her ongoing persecution was not caused by doctrinal disputes. During her interrogations she is accused of an eclectic litany of misconduct, including sedition, heresy, witchcraft, sexual debauchery, abusive behavior, dishonesty, reading abominable or fatuous books, and excessive spending on food and frivolity while in prison. Various people, often of ill-repute, cast aspersions on her personal behavior and on her relationship with La Combe. Her accusers never press formal charges, however.

Guyon consistently argues that the real, political causes of her imprisonment are systematically obscured by the public lies of her persecutors. Many quotes from the *Prison Narratives* could be provided to demonstrate this claim, but one will suffice to make the point here. In this passage, Guyon highlights the gulf between appearances and reality in the handing of her case. Regarding the forged letter attributed to La Combe, for which she was sent to the Bastille, she states:

> But what will perhaps appear incredible is that, after having spread this supposed letter from Father La Combe all over Paris and from there to the provinces, as a proof of the errors of Quietism and at the same time as a justification of the supervision that was undertaken in my case in sending me to the Bastille, neither this letter nor my relationship with Father La Combe was ever in question in all of the interrogations that I had to endure. This again is truly certain proof that they were only looking to shape opinion in the public, and even more in Rome, by mixing up the affairs with Monsieur de Cambrai with my own, in order to make him detestable to this Court. And they were looking to justify the fuss that was made through views that have nothing to do with me.[40]

Such claims are puzzling for modern readers in at least two ways. First, even at the level of appearances, how could mere intimations of sexual impropriety, let alone frivolous expenditures or entertainments, serve as the pretext for Guyon's lengthy imprisonment? Second, what role did the friendship between Guyon and Fénelon ("Monsieur de Cambrai") play among the real causes of her persecution?

Answering both of these questions requires a brief excursion into Guyon's social and cultural milieu. Society in seventeenth-century France, especially during the reign of Louis XIV, was extremely codified, ruled by strict norms of conduct designated collectively by the term '*bienséances*' (roughly, 'propriety'). Such norms depended on age, gender, social class, political and religious status, familial roles, and many other variables, but they were deeply socialized and much less fluid than in the West today. *Bienséances* defined the acceptable forms of social, political, and religious behavior. Rémy Saisslin explains that these norms of propriety were generally thought to derive from the value of conformity between the subject's behavior and its own nature. However in the Ancien Régime, such conformity came to be seen as "nothing less than the principle of imitation outside the realm of art."[41] In other words, people in various stages and conditions of life were thought to have inherent natures that determined the sorts of behavior that were appropriate for them. To live morally and to achieve happiness, especially in Guyon's time, was to act in accord with one's nature. Furthermore, since individual natures were designed to cooperate in a larger, naturally ordained political order, the peace of society as a whole was thought to depend on strict adherence to propriety. Conversely, violations of propriety constituted a public threat. Maintaining one's honor by preserving the public appearance of *bienséances* was therefore a particularly important form of civic virtue. Guyon's captors represented her as someone who did not respect *bienséances* and therefore as someone who did not conform to what was natural. Her acknowledged violations of appropriate behavior, especially her claims to apostolic authority, and her purported ones, especially her alleged sexual debauchery, were presented as evidence of a fundamentally distorted character. Each transgression ascribed to her was therefore meant to reinforce the opinion among French aristocrats that she was monstrous, dangerous, and mad.

However, Guyon's claims to spiritual advancement required one further tactic from her persecutors. Mystics, after all, were in a liminal social category, and *bienséances* became a bit blurry in such cases. It was not impossible to think that Guyon's "unnatural" actions—at least her religious teaching and healing—truly were the result of her sanctity and perhaps special divine election. The charges of frivolity and excessive spending leveled against her must therefore be understood as an attempt to exclude her from this category. Consider, for example, the following passage from an accusatory letter written by La Chétardie, her confessor in Vaugirard, which Guyon copies into Chapter 4:

Who would believe that a soul, which claims to be raised to a high level of perfection, united to God through a love so pure, and favored with the gift of contemplation and prophetic visions, might have read for over a year the news of the world at large, the newspapers of France, of Flanders, and of Holland, the journals of the Savants, the *Mercure Galant*, Aesop's Fables in verse, and novels full of amorous intrigue, of which the title alone would put off not only people who are pious, but people who are moderately well-behaved and modest?[42]

He later contrasts his worldly portrait of her with the popular idea of sainthood: "But I well know that, even in the midst of their infirmities and the harshest persecution, those whom one honors as saints still led penitent and mortified lives, that they would perform contemplative prayer ceaselessly, that they provided rare examples of patience and humility."[43]

Guyon's initial confinement in 1687 at the Visitation Sainte-Marie included extensive investigation of her mystical teachings, but she was quick to submit her writings to official judgment, and her examiners found no evidence of heresy. The same pattern repeated itself during the Issy Conferences. Her captors' subsequent disinterest in theological discussion as reported in the *Prison Narratives* seems, therefore, to be a tacit acknowledgment that they could not get what they wanted from her in this way and instead needed to focus on her alleged social transgressions. Guyon writes in the *Prison Narratives* that she fears "nothing from the truth, but only from accusations and lies."[44] Her apostolic vocation and her family situation left her very exposed to such lies. As a lay widow and mother who was also a prolific religious author and a popular teacher, she stretched many conventional social roles to the breaking point. Furthermore, as she became a spiritual counselor to many important figures at Court—including the second most important clergyman in the country—and a model of piety for the Queen of France in the late 1680s, she achieved a pinnacle of influence that was perceived as a genuine threat to the social order, and by implication to the religious and political orders as well. When she was taken to Vincennes, no members of her own family defended her; in fact, her brother had been one of her first accusers. No religious community defended her either. Her enemies could therefore make false claims about her, to accuse her by innuendo of "unspeakable" acts, to send spies to act as her servants, to attempt to poison her, to deny her medical treatment when her life was in danger, and to harass her in many other ways because of her defenselessness both inside and outside of prison.

These dynamics are clearly evident in La Chétardie's letter. He claimed to write this letter to Guyon, in order to explain his consternation at her behavior and to reassure her of his righteous intentions. In fact, though, the letter was intended for the public, for, as Guyon writes, it "ended up in newspapers of all kinds."[45] The "private" letter released to the public is a familiar rhetorical device. The purportedly private intentions of the author in such a document are meant to show the veracity of the accusations it contains. In seventeenth-century France, as discussed above, civic virtue required the individual to adhere particularly strictly to propriety in public. The result was widespread suspicion of people's behavior in public, the arena of appearances, and corresponding trust in behavior that occurred in private, the arena of reality. La Chétardie's letter took advantage of this distinction and thereby cemented the popular perception of Guyon's guilt, despite the fact that she was never actually found guilty of anything.

The relationship between Guyon and Fénelon and its role in Guyon's imprisonment can also be reinterpreted in light of their respective transgressions of *bienséances*. The deep friendship they formed between 1688 and 1690 centered on Guyon's role as spiritual mentor to Fénelon. The controversial nature of Guyon's writings and teachings made her, by association, a liability for Fénelon, especially after Madame de Maintenon turned against her in the early 1690s. Fénelon's criticisms of the King and his ongoing public dispute with Bossuet made him just as much a liability for Guyon, who considered the attacks on her reputation to be "truly certain proof that they were only looking to shape opinion in the public, and even more in Rome, by mixing up the affairs with Monsieur de Cambrai with my own, in order to make him detestable to this Court."[46] And though Fénelon's case in Rome was affected by his association with Guyon, she was even more affected by Fénelon's actions. She was imprisoned in Vincennes shortly after Fénelon's "Letter to Louis XIV" was turned over to Noailles, and she was transferred to the Bastille when Fénelon's *Telemachus* was circulated at Court. Her treatment only changed for the better when Rome condemned the *Maxims of the Saints*, thereby yielding in part to the wishes of Louis XIV. Ironically, historians have mostly sympathized with Fénelon, who is seen as having suffered and even sacrificed his reputation because he would not renounce Guyon and her various "excesses."[47] However, Guyon seems to have suffered more from the relationship, becoming a social outcast as Louis XIV punished her for Fénelon's criticisms of the regime. This interpretation of their relationship puts the responsibility for Guyon's seven-year imprisonment squarely on Fénelon's shoulders. Fénelon was "guilty" of not respecting *bienséances* by daring to criticize the King.

In this codified society Fénelon's act was considered an outrage. France in the seventeenth century was an unparalleled political power in Europe, and the primary patron of the arts and literature. Versailles represented the seat of French power, and Louis XIV, the Sun King, represented the ideal of the supreme monarch at the center of this power. As in most autocratic regimes, it was forbidden to criticize the King. The regime depended on propaganda, and its apologists were "required to write homages that in turn must not expose the great rhetorical machine; one must prove the superiority of France, of the King and of the monarchy."[48] Propaganda functions as such only when it conceals its rhetorical devices. Since these devices must remain invisible, propaganda in turn engenders censorship. It was in the best interest of the Crown not to dispute any criticism publicly. Doing so would advertise the weaknesses of the regime and, even worse, increase the chance of opposition to the King's policies among the nobility. In Fénelon's case, the King made the decision that Fénelon had to be punished painfully, but not publicly, for his breach of *bienséances*, which verged on treason. Guyon provided an alternative target for the King's revenge. According to Louis Guerrier, the method had its desired result: "the imprisonment of Mme Guyon changed everything. The Archbishop of Cambrai was profoundly afflicted by this news. He understood that they were only attacking Mme Guyon in order to get to something beyond her, and that behind Quietism there was court intrigue."[49]

If the way to attack Fénelon was through Guyon, then the way to attack Guyon was through La Combe. Since Fénelon's writings are widely considered morally courageous and praiseworthy in historical perspective, it is easy to forget that they were seen as violations of propriety. His social transgressions were overtly political and well-defined, and they solicited a quick reaction. Guyon's social transgressions derived from her claims to apostolic authority as a laywoman. These transgressions were poorly defined and difficult to prosecute, since they emerged from the long-contested social position of the mystic. Without evidence of real, uncontested impropriety on Guyon's part, her captors invented their own. As we have seen, in an environment governed by *bienséances* the slightest hint of such impropriety sufficed to raise broader suspicions about Guyon's spiritual practices. Privately, those in power understood that the issue was Fénelon's audacious criticism of the King, whereas the public believed that the issue was Guyon's misconduct with La Combe and, by implication, the moral danger lurking in her mystical writings.

Guyon and Christian Prison Literature

The final part of Guyon's account of her life is indebted to a long tradition of Christian prison literature. Since the sixteenth century at least, authors writing in this genre began to tell the stories of their imprisonment primarily as a way to present a certain idea of who they were and what they valued. In other words, in the early modern period, prison literature began to take on autobiographical characteristics. Guyon's text exemplifies this autobiographical turn. The motive for such intentional self-presentation varied with the different political and religious reasons behind the author's imprisonment. Authors writing in this genre sometimes sought freedom, martyrdom, or the consolation of loved ones. Such subjective, autobiographical intentions can arguably be found even earlier. Joanna Summers claims that "the focus upon the individualistic, the self-interested, and the political as motivation for the penning of prison texts" can be found in the prison writing of the late medieval period as well as the early modern.[50]

But for Guyon, a mystic devoted to the annihilation of the self and indifference to the personal consequences of worldly circumstances, writing in a genre devoted to self-justification or social or religious reform was fraught with difficulties. Guyon's theological convictions regarding the value and necessity of selfless suffering required her to reinterpret or depart from some of the conventional aims of autobiographical prison writing. Furthermore, Guyon's text manifests several gender-specific forms of resistance not typical of men's prison writings. We will examine these departures below by considering her motives for first writing and then suppressing this text and then by considering the text as the product of a female author. First, though, it will useful to consider some of the ways in which Guyon's writing manifests several common features of prison writing.

Clark Gilpin writes that many prison letters address a "general crisis of truth, in which traumatic events have so thoroughly disrupted the culturally received frames of reference that both the witness and those who hear the witness's story find themselves either without clear criteria of appraisal or with criteria that fail to assimilate and interpret crucial pieces of information."[51] Guyon's text struggles to articulate and overcome both a legal crisis of truth and a theological crisis of truth. Legally, she found herself shuttled between civil and religious jurisdictions,[52] denied even the semblance of due process or basic fairness, and subjected to ongoing psychological manipulation and public mockery meant to serve the political aims of her captors. Theologically, she saw her mystical writings denounced and ridiculed, had her apostolic calling suspended by her isolation, and experienced forms of suffering that were hard to interpret as spiritually beneficial. In short, "prison writing is centrally about violence," and in this text Guyon tries to understand the physical, psychological, and ideological violence she endured.[53] Like many imprisoned authors before and after her, she attempts "to overcome violence, stare death in the face and provide the basis for human affirmation."[54] We will examine this attempt below, but first it is necessary to see how she articulated the legal and theological crises created by her captivity—in a sense, to understand the questions before considering the answers.

Guyon insists throughout the text that her imprisonment and persecution were fundamentally unjust. She establishes this claim early on by way of the contrast between her treatment and the treatment of other authors condemned by the Church. Guyon explains in her *Life* how, confronted with Bossuet's condemnation of her writings, she protested her good intentions, admitted that some of her terminology was open to unorthodox interpretations, and submitted to the judgment of Church authorities.[55] The legal crisis presented in the text is occasioned by the fact that she is arrested notwithstanding her submission and pressured to confess to personal sins and heretical intentions against her conscience. She points out the double standard involved in her case: "Exactly as I said before the condemnation of my books, when bad books are written, one is content to condemn them without tormenting the people, unless they write in support of the condemned books. And, further, how should they be treated? At most, they are exiled."[56] Furthermore, while Bossuet had mocked her as "an ignorant woman who knew nothing at all," after her arrest, her persecutors treated her "with more rigor than the most skilled theologian who had committed voluntary errors on the most essential points of our faith."[57] Sometimes she expresses her legal objections with evident frustration.

> But I who have only erred concerning a few terms, according to Monsieur de Meaux himself, which do not relate to theology in the strict sense, with my not being a theologian, and only concern the matter of contemplative prayer, about which others than I have written more strongly, why should I be put in prison, I who have always submitted with all my heart? Why torment me for nearly twenty years for the same thing, when, even without requiring so many submissions and admissions of error from me, I might have abjured to protest my commitment to the church? I had always asked that my books be condemned if they were found bad and that at least I might be left in peace. I have never been able to obtain this.[58]

Guyon also protests her captors' refusal to give her a public trial with respect for basic rules of evidence. After being confined without a trial behind closed doors in Vaugirard, she asks, "Why not put me rather in the Conciergerie in the hands of Parliament? If I am guilty, I do not ask for grace, but I ask that those who spread calumny would also be punished. It is easy to accuse someone of crimes when one removes from her all means of defending herself, but in a regulated court, like the one in Parliament, the witnesses about whom they were so confident might speak differently, and at least the truth would be known." The reply of her captor constitutes a naked assertion of arbitrary power: "since the crimes that you have committed do not merit the death penalty, it is safer to keep you locked up here."[59] The Parliament of Paris in the Ancien Régime had few of the functions of a parliament in the contemporary sense of the term. It served primarily as a court of appeals for the nobility. Although it was heavily influenced by the King and permitted the use of torture in the interrogation of witnesses, Guyon nevertheless presents herself as confident that the lies of her captors were transparent enough that a trial there would expose them. She repeats her requests for a courtroom trial later, during her imprisonment in the Bastille, only to be similarly dismissed. In place of such a trial, she is interviewed for hours at a time by the Lieutenant General of Police, who records only those parts of her answers which might be deliberately misrepresented and used in a campaign to destroy her reputation. "I suffered from a very strange oppression, caused by a clever and malicious judge who had prepared his ready materials in writing, and who gave a violent twist to my responses, trying to insert his venom. Me, without defense or counsel, observed on all sides, mistreated in all ways, whom they tried to intimidate in every fashion."[60]

Guyon's theological crisis in the text centers on the question of why God permits her to suffer from the physical violence and injustice of her persecutors. Ultimately, her challenge is Job's challenge—how to interpret the personal experience of injustice and affliction. She rarely allows this question to seem like a question at all because she is so concerned to emphasize her answer to it, which is that her persecution and suffering are the means by which God purifies her of self-interest. But the question lurks behind her repeated denials of despair or even unhappiness amid the horrors of prison life. In one passage, she allows herself a very brief, understated expression of this issue as a crisis: "So much bad treatment and continual harassment saddened me to excess at certain moments, but I showed nothing. And I even reproached myself for this sadness, as unworthy of the sacrifice that I had so often made to God with my whole self and out of the love that he had given me for the cross."[61] Another passage suggests the spiritual challenge posed by her imprisonment more fully. Significantly, though, it is identical to a passage from Part 3 of her *Life*, where she presents herself as more subject to alternating spiritual advances and setbacks than she does in the *Prison Narratives*:

> And I was alone, without recourse, feeling on me the weight of the heavy hand of God, who seemed to abandon me to myself and to my own obscurity, an entire desertion within. I was unable to help myself with my natural mind, in which all vivacity had been deadened for such a long time, since I had ceased to use it in order to let myself be led by a superior mind, having worked all my life to submit my mind to Jesus Christ and my reason to his guidance. But in all this time I could not help myself, either with my reason or with any interior support, because I was like those who have never felt this admirable guidance from God's kindness and who have no natural mind. When I prayed, I only had responses of death.[62]

Guyon does try to resolve the legal and theological crises she articulates in the text. Before considering her views more fully, though, it may be useful to consider the *Prison Narratives* in light of three comparative "frames of reference" Gilpin employs in his analysis of Christian prison letters: the political, the social, and the devotional.[63]

Guyon's political frame of reference, as a prisoner in France at the height of Louis XIV's reign, was analogous in many ways to that of the seventeenth-century English prisoners Gilpin studies. Given the close association of the political and religious orders in both cases, to advance theologically heterodox beliefs was, by implication, to challenge the authority of the state. Guyon's early interrogations in prison focused on two politically loaded phrases found in letters addressed to her, as her interrogators investigated her as a threat to the state as well as the Church.[64] Thus, in England, "Throughout the period from the 1530s to 1700, the prisoner faced the daunting political problem of making a persuasive case that incarceration had resulted from innocent acts of piety, which were not covert acts of sedition and public disruption."[65] Many prisoners, including Guyon in France, sought to make this case by denying that they had subversive intentions and constructing a "counter-narrative" demonstrating their peaceful conduct and associating them with "the grand drama of salvation history as a whole," thereby universalizing their struggle and distancing it from any criticism of concrete political realities.[66]

Guyon does this by insisting on her loyalty to both the Catholic Church and the King. Confronted with theological criticism of her writings, both in Part 3 of her *Life* and in the text translated here, she repeatedly avows submission to the judgment of Church authorities and refuses to defend any unorthodox claims. Even when she criticizes the conduct of individual clergy or state officials, she is careful to qualify that criticism with statements of support for the underlying regime. For example, concerning a series of biased inquiries by Marc-René d'Argenson that she endured at the Bastille, she writes, "I said that I was appealing to Parliament, that I was asking that the affair be taken away from its current jurisdiction, and that I protested the legal invalidity of all that had happened. Never have I seen such a furor as that of Monsieur d'Argenson. He threatened me by the King. I responded to him that the King would not find it a bad thing for me to defend my innocence before this sovereign Court, and that he was too fair-minded for that."[67] Thus, the Lieutenant General of Police may receive his share of criticism in the text, but the justice of the King is never impugned.

In place of a political narrative, Guyon extends the narrative presented in Part 3 of her *Life*, according to which her persecution resulted from a conflict over competing but equally orthodox interpretations of Christian spiritual practice. She argues that she and her fellow mystics were inaugurating a new ecclesiastical era by becoming "martyrs of the Holy Spirit." Unlike the martyrs of the early Church, "These martyrs must suffer an extraordinary martyrdom, not by spilling blood but by being captives of God's will, the puppets of his providence and martyrs of his spirit. The martyrs of the primitive Church suffered for the word of God that was announced to them by the interior Word. Present-day martyrs suffer for their dependence on the Spirit of God."[68] The great danger of her time, she implies, is not a corrupted orthodoxy or an unjust government, but a widespread spiritual complacency that forfeits the great gifts of grace offered by a loving God. With this narrative she implies that her imprisonment serves neither the interests of the state nor those of the Church, but only those of the Devil who has "imprinted" his sinful "character" into fallen souls, a character that can only be erased by the activity of the Holy Spirit.[69] In the *Prison Narratives*, she amplifies this account of her situation by connecting her treatment in prison to the vicissitudes of the trial in Rome concerning Fénelon's mysticism, by repeatedly presenting the failure of her opponents to find any evidence of crime or unorthodoxy in her case, and by presenting her own peaceful and happy disposition as a constant source of frustration for her captors.

Regarding the social frame of reference in the *Prison Narratives*, Guyon again observes many conventions of prison letter writing. Her introduction to the work borrows from the epistolary form by addressing a single unknown interlocutor in the second person. The letter is meant to be shared, she says, only with "a small number of my most special friends, to whom I could not refuse this consolation, if it is one for them, who would like to learn about the views and the motives that made me suppress it for all others."[70] Taking this statement at face value, then, Guyon intended to withhold the text from publication and therefore did not expect it to spark a broader spiritual or social reform movement. Instead, she emphasizes "the bond of personal affection and common loyalty to a cause that linked the prisoner to those beyond the cell" and bears "witness to acts of representative suffering, undertaken in behalf of others, who were threatened not only by human adversaries but cosmic powers of evil and sin."[71] The "small number" of Guyon's "most special friends" probably included the members of a few French noble families who shared Guyon's mystical views—and at times even corresponded with her during her confinement at Vaugirard—and some of the international supporters who had sought her out by the time she wrote this text in 1709.

Finally, with respect to the devotional frame of reference in the text, Guyon's reflections on the spiritual meaning of her imprisonment also echo themes from other prison letters. "Prison has long served as a metaphor of life in the world and occasioned meditation on transience, fate, release from the bondage of sin, and the meaning of religious freedom. A common trope, for instance, is the notion that it is the prisoner who is becoming truly free, while those outside the walls remain 'chained' by fear, by social conformity, or by hypocrisy."[72] As is demonstrated more fully below, Guyon insists that she is happy in prison and that she enjoys a profound interior union with God that her captivity has only deepened. Conversely, she often points out the spiritual emptiness of her persecutors and describes them as being motivated by the desire for profit or social advancement. For example, speaking of her principal guard in the Bastille, she writes, "Monsieur du Junca told me, in order to excuse himself for the pain that he had caused me, that he owed his fortune to Messieurs de Noailles, of whom his father had been a servant; that he would be the governor of the Bastille after the death of Monsieur de Saint-Mars; and that he already could smell the deal. I told him that younger people often die before older ones. I could not get away from the idea that he would die before the governor. He did in fact die before him. Of what use to him was this desire for fortune? And of what use was such prudence at the expense of charity and justice?"[73]

The Private Text

Many of Guyon's departures from or reinterpretations of the conventional goals of prison writing relate to her decision not to publish this text along with the first three parts of her autobiography. If Guyon saw herself as contributing to the birth of a new era of salvation history, why did she not want more people to read about her own martyrdom to the Holy Spirit? Why did she choose such a small group of like-minded mystics as her audience? And if she claimed to transcend or even value the physical conditions of her imprisonment in pursuit of spiritual advancement, how could she simultaneously write a text that condemned those conditions? Several interesting features of the text can therefore be approached by asking why Guyon wrote such an elaborate account of her years in prison but then refused to publish it.

She claims to write out of obedience to the request of her unknown addressee ("I cannot refuse, sir, what you ask of me, and what you seem to desire with such insistence regarding the last period of my life"[74]) and, as mentioned above, out of the desire to console some of her friends. However, she also claims to have good reasons for keeping the text private. She states these reasons succinctly toward the end of Part 3 of her *Life*:

> There are details too abominable, on the part of various people, which charity makes me cover up, and it is in this sense that *charity covers a multitude of sins* (1 Pet. 4:8), and on the part of others who, being seduced by ill-intentioned people, are respectable to me for their piety and for other reasons, although they might show too bitter a zeal for things about which they really do not know. I am keeping quiet, for some of these people out of respect and for some of the others out of charity.[75]

Thus, Guyon claims to keep her narrative private out of charity for the wicked and respect for those people of good faith who were misled into collaborating in her persecution.

But, then, why did she write in the *Life* of her confinements in Paris and Meaux and the deceptions of various Church and government officials concerning her case prior to her arrest in 1695? She clarifies that she only wrote about these events to eliminate the guilt by association that had attached to her friends and family, and to clarify her orthodoxy and commitment to the Catholic Church. She writes, "it being a question of my faith for which they wanted to make me suspect, it seemed important to me to let it be known at the same time how I have always been far from the sentiments that they wanted to ascribe to me. I believed it to be my duty to religion, to piety, to my friends, to my family and to myself. But as for the bad personal treatments, I believed it necessary to sacrifice them and sanctify them through a profound silence, as I have remarked."[76]

She therefore presents her decision to write and then withhold this text as an attempt to realize competing goods: obedience to her addressee and the consolation of her friends on the one hand, and the desire to protect the privacy and reputation of her persecutors, some of whom acted in good faith or under duress, on the other. In the end, taking her stated reasons seriously and at face value helps to explain several interesting features of the text. Before exploring this thesis, however, it might be useful to consider several competing explanations of Guyon's motives.

Marie-Louise Gondal presents (and ultimately rejects) three initially plausible explanations for Guyon's decision: coquetry, indecision, or compromise between the desire to reveal what happened to her and the fear of reprisal. She suggests that writing and then withholding the text could be seen, first, as a rhetorical strategy in which the text is meant "to give itself in hiding itself— coquetry, some will certainly say." Second, this decision could be interpreted as evidence of "an incapacity to claim her own writing and, in the end, an indication of a bad conscience." Third, she might be engaged in a compromise, "invented to obey exterior pressures from opposite directions, those being to produce and publish this narrative and to suppress it. Her faithful friends would have liked it to be written and known, but the same ones or others would have liked not to awaken the old demons."[77] This third suggestion may be strengthened by recognizing that prisoners released from the Bastille had to promise never to reveal the details of their confinement.[78] If Guyon had published the text during her lifetime, she would have legally empowered any of her enemies who wished to return her to prison.

If any of these motives were determinative, however, it seems unlikely that the text would have remained undiscovered and unpublished until 1992. If Guyon was being coquettish, she could have caused the text to "give itself in hiding itself" much more effectively by allowing her friends to publish it, or at least distribute it widely, while making it appear that this action was done against her will. As for the idea that Guyon was indecisive about making her claims publicly because they were not true, or were perhaps exaggerated, it is noteworthy that she had no such indecision about the rest of her autobiography, which contains many claims, both mundane and mystical, in a similar vein. If writing but not publishing the text was an attempt to compromise between the desire to write and the fear of reprisals, then Guyon could have directed the text to be published safely enough in the Netherlands after her death, along with the rest of her *Life*.

Of course, it is possible that she wanted the text to be published posthumously but Pierre Poiret or one of the other editors who continued to publish Guyon's work after Poiret's death in 1719 withheld it against her wishes. Poiret did edit many of her other writings prior to publishing them, sometimes deleting lengthy passages. But in the case of the *Prison Narratives*, there is no evidence to confirm this hypothesis. On the contrary, Poiret's dedication to publishing Guyon's complete works and his particular appreciation of her willingness to suffer as a prisoner of conscience make it seem unlikely that he would excise this entire part of her autobiography on his own initiative.[79] There probably would have been a strong international readership for the text in the eighteenth century, since "the early foreign reputation of Madame Guyon and Fénelon was as martyrs to Louis' political and religious policies."[80]

Gondal argues that Guyon's compulsion to write this text is very typical of her need "to deliver her life, from day to day, to the fire of Justice, the incandescent lava of which burns all—she who experiences it as much as those who seek to protect it" (Gondal 19). While this is a more promising suggestion, it serves more as an explanation of why she would write the text than of why she would withhold it from publication. By considering the coherence of Guyon's own stated motives with the primary emphases of the text as written, the answer to the rest of the puzzle becomes clearer. Such considerations can also provide a useful framework for interpreting the text.

In the opening paragraph, she claims to write primarily for the "consolation" of her friends and supporters and, by implication, denies that her motive is self-interested. In particular, she does not wish to be seen as challenging the official account of her case or seeking to restore her public reputation. Since "opprobrium and ignominy" are two of the chief means by which God brings about her (spiritually salutary) suffering, it would seem to be spiritually counterproductive—by her own measure—to mitigate those means by justifying herself. In what sense could this text provide a "consolation" to its readers, circulated as it was after she had already been freed? First, it could show them that their loyalty was not misplaced, since the rumors that were publicly circulated to destroy Guyon's reputation were false. Guyon speaks to this concern when discussing her reasons for accepting the offer of release from the Bastille: "But what made me determined [to leave] more than the rest was the belief that, my conduct justifying me in the future, my friends would also be justified by the kindness they have shown me, because, as my dear Master said to his disciples: 'I sanctify myself for them' (John 17:19)."[81] Second, it could show them that her persecution did not destroy her, and that, in fact, she considered herself closer to God as a result of it. In this way they might be liberated from feelings of guilt or inadequacy due to their failure to obtain her release sooner. Third, communicating the unknown truth about her years of imprisonment could deepen the intimacy between Guyon and her readers. By extension, she probably hoped they would be inspired to continue teaching and observing the devotional practices she championed. She says as much in the closing pages: "For my principal reason for writing this—when death might appear at any instant to end my destiny, and with my no longer claiming anything on earth except you, O my Lord, and you alone—has been the glory of God, and that contemplative prayer might not be harmed by accusing those who sincerely practice it of crimes."[82]

If these were Guyon's true motives, sharing this text privately with her friends would seem to be the only strategy that could succeed. To publish the text might lessen her public disgrace, but doing so would seriously undermine the claim that she embraced that very disgrace as a divine gift. It would also open her experience to public scrutiny in a way that would preclude its use in cementing the private bonds of friendship. Merely circulating the text among the members of her inner circle, in contrast, maintained her public disgrace while satisfying their concerns.

With respect to her legacy this decision was one of the most important she ever made. By refusing to seek a public self-justification, she permitted her own marginalization in mainstream French history while founding a subcultural movement on the authority of her own martyrdom. Many of her most important followers were particularly devoted to her because of the spiritual authenticity they perceived in her response to her persecution.[83] The emergence of this text, complete with its declaration of intentional self-suppression, helps to explain this devotion.

Self-Justification and Self-Annihilation

Guyon's stated objective for the text is not easy to accomplish. How does one unmask the lies of one's oppressors and thus console one's friends while simultaneously maintaining one's own disinterest in the personal consequences of those lies? Does not Guyon's very act of unmasking these lies represent a self-justification, rather than an acceptance of suffering in disgrace—even if the justification only occurs in the minds of her friends? Simply writing the *Prison*

Narratives might imply, in the minds of some readers, that she has contradicted her own profession of spiritual equanimity: "I can want neither justification nor esteem. If God wants one or the other, he will do as he wishes; it does not matter to me. Let him glorify himself through my destruction or in reestablishing my reputation; either one or the other is equal on the scale."[84] She attempts to avoid this implication by repeatedly differentiating two sets of concerns in the text: her audience's and her own. Paralleling these two sets of concerns, she deploys two alternative guiding narratives to present the Christian meaning of her prison experience. The result is a fascinating division in the voice of the narration.

When speaking to the concerns of her audience—primarily, the "consolation" of her friends—she reports the abusive conditions of her confinement and the lack of judicial process or even minimal fairness in the prosecution of her legal case. Guyon's narrative task in addressing these concerns is to unmask her oppressors and to refute their lies. In a sense, she does aim to justify herself and demonstrate her innocence, but, she insists, not for her own sake. She must do so only in order that her friends might rest easy in their association with her and share in the knowledge of this important and formative period of her life. The Christian narrative guiding this self-portrayal is implicitly a prophetic one—the denunciation of unjust imprisonment as dehumanizing, cruel, unjust, and scandalous. She carries out this task simply by presenting and criticizing her treatment in detail, rather than drawing explicitly from the Prophets (although she does quote Jeremiah 7:33 in Chapter 3).[85]

In addressing these concerns, she presents a steady stream of details about the everyday absurdities and insults of prison life, the farcical machinations of her oppressors, and the casual brutality she experienced. Some of the vignettes she presents have an almost surreal, Kafkaesque quality, especially when she includes reports of her dreams in the narrative.[86] Consider, for example, the false piety of her chief tormentor in Vaugirard, Joachim Trotti de La Chétardie. She describes their first meeting as follows: "He came to me then, and, falling to his knees as soon as he had entered my chamber, he spent a quarter of an hour in prayer without speaking a single word to me. This beginning and this pretentiousness made a certain impression of fear on me that was only proven true later on."[87] After he fails to procure an admission of heresy from her, she writes, "Sometime later the parish priest, who no longer performed his prayers, came back, but with an air full of anger."[88] Still later, he is presented as a deceptive bully: "I never heard him say a true word or the same thing twice; he was always confused, often speaking through his teeth like a man who threatens and who does not want to speak clearly about things."[89]

Through these descriptions, Guyon criticizes his abuse of the priestly office, particularly since she was obliged to confess to him. After several intensely unpleasant encounters, Guyon alludes to the inappropriateness of his priestly clothing, writing, "I had terrible dreams about him; sometimes I would see him vomit a black substance on me, and at other times it seemed to me that our Lord made him take off his clothes and clothed him in another, dirty way."[90]

She sums up and criticizes the injustice and meanness of the Bastille in a succinct, powerful paragraph:

> You are made to experience only what can bring you pain in this place and nothing that can bring you pleasure. You only see terrible faces, which only treat you most harshly. You are without defense when you are accused. They circulate rumors on the outside as they want. In other prisons you have counsel if you are accused; you have lawyers in order to defend yourself and judges who, in examining the truth, enlighten one another. But here, you have no one. You have only one judge, who is most often judge and jury, as has happened to me, who interrogates you as he pleases, who writes down whatever he wants from your answers, and who is free from all rules of justice, and there is no one at all who corrects him afterwards. They try to persuade you that you are guilty; they make you believe that there are a lot of things against you.[91]

Many more passages could be quoted that offer detailed observations and criticisms of Guyon's treatment in prison. In fact, such passages comprise the bulk of the text. Interestingly, though, her pursuit of self-justification is not only the primary selection principle by which she determines what to include in the narrative. It also shapes her underlying rhetorical framework.

Guyon structures her text to create a contrast between the rhetoric of deception and public manipulation used by her oppressors, and the rhetoric of truth and private sincerity in her own writing. The first half of the narrative culminates in La Chétardie's long letter full of accusations against her, which she copies into Chapter 4. She organizes the chapters leading up to this letter to refute most of its claims in advance, so that when readers arrive at it, they are already sympathetic to her perspective on the charges it contains. She uses a similar strategy in the subsequent chapters concerning life in the Bastille, presenting her version of events first, then reporting the calumnies spread by her enemies about the events she has already narrated. The attacks against

Guyon, spread in the papers and by rumor, did not present her primarily as a doctrinal or political threat, but instead as a ridiculous figure. While claiming great spiritual elevation and sanctity, these attacks suggested, Guyon spent her money recklessly in pursuit of frivolous entertainments and sensual pleasures. She (and by extension Fénelon and other mystics in her circle) were hypocrites—Tartuffes. By presenting her version of events first, and in great detail, she shows the intentional deceptions used to make such slander seem plausible. For example, the letter accuses her of spending excessively on expensive food while confined in Vaugirard, but before her readers reach this accusation, Guyon has already explained her side of the story:

> The parish priest, who normally gave her [the nun living with Guyon] room and board, instead put the money into her hands and prohibited her to give me a cent, but told her to give me what I needed generously and to write it down. They began by making me buy game, which I do not eat at all, and many other things, so as to make people think that I lived extravagantly, and they would be able to use that later to decry me and make me out to be a sensual person. When I asked them to buy me meat from the butcher that I like a lot, they could not get it, and they made me buy so many chickens that, not being able to eat them, I let them become hens, of which there remain a great quantity, as well as young chicks.

Including La Chétardie's letter within her own narrative also gives the appearance of fair-mindedness, since she is willing to let her accuser's voice be heard on its own terms.

Guyon adopts a strikingly different tone and evokes a different biblical narrative in the brief passages of the text in which she reflects on the meaning of her prison experiences. When addressing her own concerns she repeats her own indifference to, and even gratitude for, her circumstances. For example, speaking of her attitude after Fénelon's *Maxims of the Saints* had been officially (though mildly) condemned in Rome, she writes, "They believed without a doubt that I would say that an injustice had been done to him, and that, having shown more force in supporting him than myself, I would display extreme chagrin and a fit of anger. But they saw the same equanimity toward this as toward the rest. They asked this young woman whom they had put with me if I was not truly sad. She responded no."[92] Her isolation becomes prayerful solitude: "My solitude was so sweet, having a girl with me from whom I hid nothing and with whom I could pray and stay silent when it pleased me, that, without the perpetual interrogations that I had to suffer, I would have preferred prison to all the delights of life because my pleasure cannot be in these things, but in God. The ability to find him without being subjected to seeing or speaking to creatures was luxurious to me."[93] Her pain, exhaustion, and disgrace simply conform her spirit more fully to Christ's spirit. Even in the face of death, she repeatedly frustrates her tormentors with the consistency of her happy disposition, sustained as it is by permanent and lasting union with God. And in many passages she even claims to prefer prison to freedom: "I had neither the idea nor the desire to leave prison. I had imagined myself staying there for the rest of my life. The thought of staying alone there made me very happy. I felt myself become weaker every day, and I waited for the end of my life with delight."[94] She accordingly casts this period of her life as a demonstration of her earlier claims of spiritual advancement through the complete annihilation of the self and resulting abandonment to the will of God.

Her guiding theological narrative in addressing the meaning of her imprisonment in relation to her own well-being is thus the story of the cross. Her experiences of public humiliation, physical suffering, and confinement allow her to adhere all the more closely to the victim-state of Christ crucified. In doing so, she participates more fully in the mystical transformation to new life made possible by the death and resurrection of Jesus. The opening and closing paragraphs of the text emphasize this self-sacrificial narrative. In her brief introduction, Guyon writes that during this period of her life, "God made [her] most a part of his cross," and she "was, like [her] dear Master, filled with opprobrium and ignominy." Her last sentence states, "I do not doubt that my dear Master will save up fiercer and stronger, though less dazzling, crosses for me, until the end of my days."

Guyon's presentation of the meaning of her prison experiences is therefore fairly one-dimensional with respect to her own spiritual growth. As discussed above, her singularity of spiritual purpose in the *Prison Narratives* helps to explain her shift away from the lengthy introspective digressions that are so characteristic of the first three parts of the *Life*. In one passage she does break from her account of the events of prison life to reflect on their theological meaning. Unsurprisingly, the passage directly concerns her participation, by her suffering, in the cross of Christ:

I would sometimes say, "As for my particular situation, what does it matter to me what men think of me; what does it matter what they make me suffer, since they cannot separate me from Jesus Christ, who is engraved at the bottom of my heart. If I displease Jesus Christ, though I might please all men, it would make me less than mud. Let all men therefore scorn me and hate me, provided that I am agreeable to him. Their blows will polish what is defective in me so that I may be presented to the one for whom I die every day, until he comes to consummate this death." And I would pray to you, O my God, to make me an offering pure and clean in your blood, so as to be offered to you.[95]

This passage is also found in Part 3 of the *Life*. There are no dramatic transitions from one spiritual state to another here, no discoveries of novel forms of prayer, mission, or virtue. These transitions and discoveries are the central elements of her published autobiography. They are replaced here with the brute realities of suffering and the consistent response of faith, which recur throughout the narrative.

What is the response of faith, according to Guyon? It is to offer one's suffering as a sacrifice to God and to embrace it as a form of purification that destroys self-reliance and makes those who suffer more like Christ in their dependence on God. In her *Short and Easy Method of Prayer*, Guyon presents this view, which is also repeated in many of her other writings:

> Be happy about all that God will make us suffer. If you love him, you must love him on Calvary just as on Mount Tabor, since it is the place where he makes love most evident.... As soon as you find something that discourages you and brings on suffering, first offer it up to God, and then give yourself up as a sacrifice. You will see that when the cross comes, it will not be as heavy as you would have thought. This does not mean that you will not feel its weight. Some imagine that the only suffering is that of the cross. But actually to feel suffering is one of the very principles of suffering. Jesus Christ wanted to suffer in the most painful way. Sometimes we carry the cross with weakness, at other times with strength. All should be equal.[96]

Similar ideas can be found in the work of many other imprisoned Christian writers. As Ioan Davies points out, "That prison might provide a discipline which is conducive to clear thinking and internal control has been argued by many people, none more so than those religious writers to whom the practices of abstinence, self-mortification, poverty and hardship are virtues in themselves."[97] Gilpin notes that many sixteenth-century authors imprisoned in England shared the view that "resolute adherence to Christian faith carried with it suffering for conscience and that suffering gave evidence of resolute faith."[98] This theme is grounded in the Bible, especially the crucifixion narratives in the Gospels and Paul's accounts of his imprisonment, but also the Psalms, the story of Shadrach, Meshach, and Abednego presented in Daniel 3, and other Old Testament texts. For Guyon, however, the theme is taken to a self-annihilating extreme. Suffering is not merely a frequent accompaniment or sign of faith in her theology, but rather the integral means God uses to purify the soul of its selfish desires and prepare it for divine union.[99] If the soul does not experience such suffering in this life to the point that it loses all merely personal preferences, it must do so in purgatory.[100]

Guyon's valorization of suffering produces an interesting narrative result. She is ultimately released from the Bastille. Prison narratives often present the captive's release as redemption from the injustice of confinement and persecution, perhaps even a vindication of her moral or theological rectitude. In contrast, Guyon's insistence on the spiritual necessity and value of suffering makes it impossible for her to tell such a story. Prison must be, at least as far as spiritual well-being is concerned, as fitting a place to suffer as any other. Indeed, there is no climactic celebration after her release. Instead, in the brief closing pages of the narrative, she describes a new and even more oppressive suffering in her son's household. Even later, after moving to her own residence, she endures further suffering in the prison of her own ailing body. There is no ultimate release from suffering in this life, Guyon seems to say, nor should one wish for one, so long as the faithful are called to share fully in the cross of Christ.

Although this rhetorical strategy—the differentiation of her concerns from those of her audience—is consistent, at least in principle, the two sets of responses to prison life are nonetheless in tension with each other. As already mentioned, Guyon spends much more time in the *Prison Narratives* recounting the external events of her persecution and demonstrating the unfairness and malice of her persecutors than she does communicating her spiritual response. The result is that her pursuit of self-justification and her prophetic denunciations of an unjust legal system (for her friends' sake) tend to outweigh her claim to selfless disinterest in her own earthly condition. Her avowals of contentment and equanimity in the face of suffering may therefore ring hollow for some readers against the pervasive narrative self-exoneration that structures the text. One of the most interesting aspects of the *Prison Narratives*, however, is that Guyon seems aware of this tension and sometimes seeks to resolve it. The opening and closing pages are exemplary in this respect. Ultimately, her decision to exclude this text from the version of her *Life* meant for publication can be seen as an essential component of her rhetorical strategy—the proof that her stated motives are sincere. The text, as intentionally and necessarily private, can therefore be seen as a creative attempt to present the simultaneous vindication and destruction of the self.

Guyon and Women's Prison Writings

Guyon's narrative is one of the earliest examples of a prison memoir written by a woman. Such texts were extremely unusual before the late eighteenth century. Not only had prisons not been widely used for long-term confinement before then, but few incarcerated women were literate.[101] Given the similarities discussed above between this narrative and other prison writings (most authored by men), it might seem that Guyon's gender does not play a particularly important role in the text. However, further reflection on some of the distinctive features of women's prison writing suggests otherwise. In order to explore the extent to which Guyon's writing shares concerns characteristic of other female prison writers, in this section we consider her *Prison Narratives* in conversation with the work of Elissa Gelfand.

Gelfand argues that there are significant differences between women's and men's prison literature. One of the key differences she notes is that male prisoners wrote in pursuit of the purportedly "universal" goal of social change—a goal that did not overtly concern their individual cases or reputations—while the women she studied did not explicitly address these "universal" issues. Instead, these women claimed to accept the given social order while subversively contesting its construction of femininity in the way they presented themselves. Gelfand writes, "male prison literature, long assumed to be 'universal' because it challenged society as a whole, in fact reflects each author's highly individual search for transcendence and change. Conversely, the female tradition, deemed 'particular' because its authors apparently affirmed their personal conformity, ultimately shows how women exploited and manipulated prevailing social and criminological discourse to counter general myths about women criminals."[102] As an extension of this difference, Gelfand suggests that male prison writers tend to present themselves as heroic in the way they reject and overcome the prevailing social order, by offering a vision of either "spiritual enlightenment or social liberation" in their writing.[103] In contrast, she claims, women have generally not sought to transcend the social forces responsible for their imprisonment by appealing to a higher moral or spiritual order: "For imprisoned women, mind and body have never existed in this same relationship; rather, their corporality has been emphasized, as it has been for all women, and their potential for transcendence has therefore been limited or denied."[104] In some ways the gendered aspects of Guyon's prison writings can be fruitfully explored in light of Gelfand's generalizations, but in other ways Guyon defies those generalizations. Gelfand's observations are based primarily on the texts of female prisoners writing in post-Revolutionary France. Some of the differences between Guyon and these authors can be explained by cultural shifts that took place over the course of the eighteenth century concerning mysticism and femininity, but other differences result from Guyon's unique social situation.

Like the authors Gelfand examines, Guyon is centrally concerned to counter the official portrayal of her identity, which emphasized her transgression of socially accepted gender roles. Thus, Guyon shares the need of these authors to show that their "'true' identity—and this presentation of self is the prime topos of women's prison literature—did not lie in judicial or criminal labels."[105] The first and perhaps most important element of the official portrayal of Guyon as a criminal concerned her sexual morality. Gelfand writes, concerning the eighteenth century, "With the growing consolidation of the couple and the definition of feminine honor in terms of conjugal fidelity, notions of a 'dangerous' or 'suspect' woman centered on her family role.... Thus widows, orphans, and vagabond and exiled women, by their rootless sexual status, were the most vulnerable to accusation and the most severely punished."[106] Guyon, of course, was widowed at the age of 28 and never remarried. Her relationship with her confessor, François La Combe, was the subject of salacious innuendo for most of the rest of her life and played an important role in her imprisonment. In the *Prison Narratives*, she presents her opponents as seeking to tarnish her sexual reputation publicly and thereby to discredit the form of mysticism she advocated: "He [Louis-Antoine de Noailles, Archbishop of Paris] wanted to have me make a public declaration that I had committed all kinds of shameful debaucheries with Father La Combe and made terrible threats against me if I did not declare that I had imposed on good people, that I had tricked them and that I was engaged in debauchery when I had done my writing."[107] She takes great pains to show that the letter purportedly written by La Combe suggesting a sexual relationship between them was a forgery. She also addresses similar accusations published during her confinement in a memoir by Dom Innocent Le Masson, an associate of her old enemy, the Bishop of Geneva, and she is deeply insulted when she hears a worker at the convent in Vaugirard voice his opinion that "there must be some women of ill repute locked up in this house."[108]

Gelfand's observations suggest, rightly, a striking difference between Guyon's non-confrontational response to the sexual conventions motivating this type of accusation and the response of another famous inmate of the Bastille, the Marquis de Sade, whose imprisonment served as the occasion for his attack on mainstream morality and piety. Guyon asserts her conformity to gendered expectations of female sexual constraint by emphatically denying these accusations. She does, however, implicitly contest the gender-based double standard implied by them. While other controversial (male) religious writers are investigated solely on the basis of their orthodoxy and civic loyalty, Guyon suggests, she is subject to ongoing, unproven and fabricated allegations about her personal sexual conduct without any opportunity for a fair defense.

Another important gender-specific accusation addressed in the text is that Guyon has claimed an improper authority to teach about spiritual matters. As Gelfand points out, "submissiveness became the most valued sign of female normality. And a criminal act, seen as the strongest form of self-assertion, was considered the complete refusal of women's passivity and the denial of their assigned role."[109] Guyon presents and responds to such accusations in several places. She reports that one of the nuns who guarded her in Vaugirard had been interrogated by La Chétardie about whether she ever presumed to preach dogma. When this nun tells him that Guyon sometimes discussed readings about the lives of the saints with her, he replies, "She preached dogma, and that is all that I wanted."[110] The letter she copies in the text, which she claims was written by La Chétardie, also includes this accusation: "why do you get mixed up in preaching dogma, teaching, and publicizing your new doctrines in the Church, which you see causing such scandals here? Let yourself be silent, in accord with the established order of the Apostle, so as to learn the orthodox doctrine, especially as a teacher, as you have done only too much."[111]

In this case, too, she explicitly defends her conformity to culturally received notions of femininity, while implicitly resisting them in her self-presentation. In the very first chapter of her narrative, she reports signing an official submission to the judgment of Church officials concerning her work. She repeats similar sentiments throughout the text: "The parish priest...put this submission in my hands. It held essentially that I had never strayed from the sentiments of the Catholic Church, my mother, for whom I always had, have now and, by the grace of God, will have all my life all possible commitment, and that if my ignorance had made me use less precise terms, my feelings have always been righteous, etc. For, in the end, whatever persecution might have been leveled against me, everything has always revolved around these terms. I signed the paper as they brought it to me."[112] Guyon's resistance to the norm of female submissiveness, at least with regard to mystical teaching, is quite explicit in some of her earlier writing—especially the third part of her autobiography.[113] In her *Prison Narratives*, though, it is more subtle and fits Gelfand's model quite well. She presents her happiness and acceptance of suffering in the text as the ultimate illustration of the mystical system she spent most of her life teaching. Her very avowals of doctrinal and physical submission to authority therefore demonstrate the authenticity of her spiritual claims regarding the path to selflessness and imply her corresponding authority to communicate those claims to others. Even more important, the very act of writing and sharing the text enacts this authority performatively. Again, therefore, Guyon's response to criticisms of her claim to spiritual authority demonstrates Gelfand's pattern—explicit acceptance of the social and ideological order combined with resistance embedded in a coded, subversive self-presentation.

Although Guyon certainly exemplifies the concern with feminine identity that Gelfand finds in other female prison writers, she also demonstrates some of the characteristics that Gelfand associates exclusively with male authors. Gelfand writes, "In opposition to the upward movement found in most men's texts—movement toward spiritual enlightenment or social liberation—the moral and social 'fall' that characterizes most women's texts does not reflect the same vision. This fatalistic mode in women's plots ran counter to the heroism that informed men's stories."[114] In contrast, Guyon's text is decidedly heroic and presents visions of both spiritual enlightenment and social liberation in response to her prison experience.

As demonstrated above, Guyon presents a contentious religious vision in the *Prison Narratives*, but not one that challenges the content of doctrinal orthodoxy or the legitimacy of the Church's sacerdotal authority. Instead, she contests the spiritual complacency of the laity and advocates a path to spiritual development and union with God meant to complement conventional morality and participation in the sacraments. Guyon presents her spiritual teachings in other writings much more fully than she does in this text, but here they are put to their strongest test and shown by her own example to be the only way to overcome the despair and constant threat of death inherent in prison life. In the Bastille, she writes, "the poor people who do not know what faith in God or abandonment to his will are, and who moreover feel guilty, grow desperate."[115] Gelfand argues that women prison writers typically do not contest or seek to transcend the prevailing order by appealing to religion: "Even the potential for transcendence and for the 'unawareness of self' that religion provides…has not served women. Paradoxically, though women have historically been closer than men to religion and mysticism, these influences have been too real and concrete to permit liberation and have, in fact, impeded women's spiritual escape."[116] Given her repeated rejection of the values of her oppressors and her own claims to a liberating spiritual equanimity in the midst of suffering, Guyon seems a clear exception to this generalization.

Guyon also offers a modest vision of social liberation. As mentioned above, when she addresses the concerns of her audience, she often presents indictments of the cruelty and injustice of her incarceration. Certainly, some of her critiques tend toward the subjective, focusing on the ways that her case in particular was handled without respect for the rule of law and how it represented an exception to the ordinary (and presumably fairer) treatment of other prisoners. Such subjective concern without explicit social contestation is what a generalization of Gelfand's observations would predict: "The texts that follow [by female authors], despite the noble and stirring expectations of domination, power, and transcendence found in critical studies of prison writing, do not reorganize experience in an attempt to shatter or correct the world. Any such 'muscle' is self-consciously ironic or offhand. Nor do these texts display a consistent judgment of the world: their anger shows private ambivalence rather than unbridled energy. And they do not offer an alternative vision of society: they wrestle with the primary act of self-expression."[117] Despite her concern with the injustice of her own treatment, in contrast, Guyon sometimes also issues broader criticisms of the prison system or state officials, although, as mentioned above, she consistently maintains her loyalty to the King. Such social criticism is most evident in her depiction of the psychologically abusive treatment of her fellow prisoners in the Bastille and her presentation of their resulting despair and hopelessness.

There are several plausible explanations for Guyon's divergence from the more typically subjective, coded, and subversive model of women's prison writing Gelfand presents. First, as a wealthy female prisoner of conscience, Guyon was extremely atypical. For women, "crime in general was almost synonymous with poverty, vagabondage, and prostitution. Patterns in female crime reveal it to be domestic or economic in nature."[118] In contrast, the grounds for Guyon's imprisonment were ultimately ideological, despite the subsequent attempts of her oppressors to portray her as a seditious sectarian leader or a sexual libertine. Her privileged socioeconomic status gave her the leisure and freedom to challenge prevailing assumptions about mysticism and prayer and about women's authority to offer spiritual instruction. As a seventeenth-century woman writing, traveling, and teaching about religious matters outside the convent system, and doing so, moreover, without the protections afforded by marriage, she was almost unique. Her ability to defy conventional gender roles in this way depended heavily on the security provided by her wealth and her powerful friends at Court. When some of these friends turned against her, she became vulnerable. Guyon's defiance of conventional spiritual practices began well before her imprisonment, however, and her extension of this defiance through her prison writings was therefore quite natural. Gelfand writes, "Given the crimes women were most likely to commit and be punished for—quotidian, banal, domestic ones—it was impossible for them to cast themselves in the heroic mold."[119] Conversely, given Guyon's life history, her sense of apostolic mission, and her ideologically grounded imprisonment, it was almost impossible for her not to present herself as a hero and martyr of the mystical movement.

The likelihood that women might contest social or religious norms on the basis of mystical authority also decreased dramatically in France after Guyon's imprisonment. During the seventeenth century, a number of French women attained informal positions of spiritual authority by virtue of their personal mystical experiences. Most of these women taught within the cloisters of monastic orders, but some, such as Madame Acarie and Jane de Chantal, found creative ways to reinterpret the gender roles and monastic rules of their time so as to teach more freely. As mentioned above, Guyon extended her claim of spiritual authority even further, refusing to accept a monastic appointment (after being pressured to become the superior of the New Catholics in Gex), traveling and engaging in itinerant spiritual teaching, and writing manuals of spiritual instruction as well as biblical commentaries. Her rejection of the traditional institutions used to control women's religious authority was one important cause of her imprisonment. However, Guyon's own persecution and the Quietist Affair more broadly had a chilling effect on the wellspring of such claims to authority, since, as a result of these events, "The eighteenth century saw the almost complete rout in France of Catholic mysticism, which without completely disappearing remained concealed."[120] As women's mystical writing and teaching became increasingly viewed, first, as dangerous and unorthodox and, later, as evidence of madness or hysteria, this path to female religious authority became correspondingly inaccessible in French Catholicism. Mysticism became even more culturally marginalized by the growing secularism of the post-Revolutionary period. It is therefore not surprising to discover a sharp difference between Guyon and the French female prison writers who came after her, with respect to their willingness to criticize the powers that imprisoned them by appealing to a higher order of values grounded in religious experience.

Conclusion

Guyon's public silence and private eloquence concerning her long imprisonment produced a divided legacy. On the one hand, her imprisonment and the public inaccessibility of her account of it led to her marginalization in France—first, during her lifetime and, later, among French historians. On the other hand, among her international readers who were more critically disposed toward the French regime, her imprisonment cemented her status as a religious and political martyr. Although it is impossible to know how widely her *Prison Narratives* circulated among these readers, it does seem likely from manuscript evidence that multiple copies were made. It also seems likely that this text, and perhaps an oral tradition based on it, enhanced her international reputation. Changes in French theology after the Quietist Affair also deepened the division between the perception in France of Guyon as an unstable heretic and international perceptions of Guyon as a sanctified martyr. As mentioned above, Guyon's persecution marked the end of the mainstream Catholic mystical tradition in France. Without a sustainable community of followers to defend her ideas there, her personal treatment in historical accounts became a matter of indifference. However, her social, political, and theological displacement from French society enhanced her international status. Guyon's Protestant followers reinterpreted her as an unwitting exile unmoored from, or even opposed to, the religious and social contexts into which she was born and lived and thereby liberated themselves to search for their own heterodox ideas in her books.

Patricia Ward has recently traced the paths by which Guyon's influence spread outside of France, especially in Holland, Scotland, England, Germany, and America.[121] In Amsterdam in 1704 Pierre Poiret began publishing and disseminating her writings, which ultimately comprised 40 volumes, and he was particularly responsible for the spread of her ideas in Holland. Guyon simultaneously maintained an extensive correspondence with leaders of various spiritual movements in the countries where she was becoming known, including self-identified Quietists, Quakers, and Pietists. The mystical author Andrew Michael Ramsey generated interest in her spiritual teachings in Scotland. Guyon became increasingly influential among Pietists after many of her writings were translated into German in the 1720s, and, more importantly, after Johann Friedrich Haug integrated much of her biblical commentary into the Berleburg Bible. The story of Guyon's early influence in England and North America is too complex to summarize here, but the central characters are German Pietist immigrants and Quakers in Pennsylvania who translated many of her works into English and published them in widely read spiritual anthologies. Later in the eighteenth century, John Wesley's inclusion of Guyon's "A Mother's Advice to Her Daughter" in his *Christian Library* gave her a readership among Methodists.

In France, Guyon was silenced physically through her imprisonment and as an author through the condemnation of her books. She also chose to remain silent about the Quietist Affair by withholding the *Prison Narratives* from publication.[122] Popular perceptions of her were therefore shaped by the slander of her enemies published in newspapers and in books by Bossuet and Dom Innocent Le Masson. Voltaire expressed a view of Guyon that was widespread in France in the eighteenth century when he wrote that Guyon was "a woman without worth, without really any intellect, and who only had an excitable imagination."[123] This perspective was essentially uncontested in French scholarship through the end of the nineteenth century. The description of Guyon in a thesis from 1850 entitled *Sur la Controverse de Bossuet et de Fénelon sur le Quiétisme* is typical:

> Near the end of the year 1687, a woman [Guyon] who still had traces of youth and beauty, and a name associated with wealth, and who even held on to alliances and relationships to all of the most illustrious at the Court of France, was arrested in Paris by the order of the King and accused of a correspondence with the head of the Quietists, and of holding gatherings where she preached this new doctrine, after having sought to spread it through small published texts, and through writings passed from hand to hand with a mystery that only made them more dangerous. We must not commit the offense of ignoring a woman who was able to keep the esteem and friendship of Fénelon, who in turn was able to ignore for a few years the judgment of Bossuet, in the history of Quietist Controversy. But neither must we do her the honor of delving into her writings and looking for a doctrine, a system, there.[124]

By the end of the nineteenth century and into the twentieth, some scholars began to offer more balanced treatments of her, including Louis Guerrier,

Henri Bremond, Henri Delacroix, Louis Cognet, Jean Orcibal, and Jean-Robert Armogathe. This tradition continues today with the work of Marie-Louise Gondal, Jacques Le Brun, Marie-Florine Bruneau, and Dominique Tronc.

However, the results of Guyon's silence and her silencing are still discernible among some contemporary scholars who adopt elements of the hostile narrative imposed on her during her lifetime and perpetuate her reputation as a threat to the established political order of her time. She is often presented as a particularly harmful influence on Fénelon. When her theology is mentioned, Bossuet's judgment of Guyon as a "heretic" is often repeated, even though she submitted to the Articles of Issy.[125] Consider Max Gallo's recent history of the last half of Louis XIV's reign. Gallo's presentation of Guyon echoes Voltaire's attitude toward her and attacks her integrity and theology, even implicating her sexual morality. Gallo calls her "a strange mystic"[126] who spiritually seduced certain powerful women at Court with her spiritual theatrics and who was even crafty enough to trick the wise and revered Bossuet.[127] He argues that the King lost confidence in the sage advice of Madame de Maintenon, upon whom he had deeply depended, because she had been taken in by Guyon and Fénelon.[128] His account also implies that Guyon and her followers were indirectly responsible for increasingly frequent public comments suggesting that Madame de Maintenon was a religious hypocrite of shallow piety.[129]

Guyon received much friendlier treatment among German and English writers as her spiritual works quickly became a major influence in the development of transatlantic Protestant piety.[130] It is plausible to think that a small but influential circle of this movement's early leaders read her private *Prison Narratives* and thereby deepened their devotion to the woman whom many considered their spiritual mother. Her followers in Blois were committed to her while she lived and to her writings after she died. It was through them that her work gained widespread readership among Quakers, Pietists, and Methodists in the eighteenth and nineteenth centuries. Guyon's role in Court politics was clearly subordinate for these readers to her importance as a spiritual teacher and author. Thomas Cogwell Upham's popular nineteenth-century biography of Guyon illustrates these priorities well.[131] English translations of her writings continue to inspire many contemporary evangelical and charismatic Christians. These audiences read their own theological concerns into her life and teachings no less than her early followers did. Today, popular Christian presses present her as a kind of "honorary Protestant" and an exemplar of personal sanctification.[132] In North America, in particular, she is still widely considered a model evangelical Christian whose writings testify to the value of a personal relationship with Jesus Christ and the necessity of suffering and the conviction of sin for achieving transformation by the Holy Spirit.[133]

Hopefully, this translation of Guyon's *Prison Narratives* will inspire still further reinterpretation of the life and work of this controversial and fascinating author. For English-speaking readers the text may reinforce certain received notions about Guyon. For example, her mystical theology in the work is quite consistent with her other writings, as she advocates self-abandonment brought about by contemplative prayer and purifying suffering. It should also bring to light elements largely ignored or dismissed by English-speaking readers. Guyon was an important person in the French Court who wielded significant influence over many of the most powerful figures in seventeenth-century France, including the King and Queen and members of notable aristocratic families. She was also a woman whose itinerant teaching defied the reigning norms of female propriety. The causes of her persecution, according to her own account, resulted more from these political entanglements and social transgressions than from her theological claims. This and the fact that she always remained a devout Catholic who saw her mystical writings as an expression of a proper and traditional form of piety make it difficult to understand her as a crypto-Protestant suffering for her opposition to orthodoxy. Perhaps those who hear Guyon speaking in this narrative after 300 years of silence will be encouraged to embrace these and other new understandings of her legacy.

The Prison Narratives
The Prisons, An Autobiographical Account

[1.] I cannot refuse, sir, what you ask of me, and what you seem to desire with such insistence regarding the last period of my life, which was that in which God made me most a part of his cross, and concerning which I can say that I was, like my dear Master, filled with opprobrium and ignominy. I believed it necessary to suppress some of the story of my life, which I was asked to write. I have explained the reasons,[1] and they would still make me keep silent if I had not been persuaded that what remains for me to say will be solely for you and a small number of my most special friends, to whom I could not refuse this consolation, if it is one for them, who would like to learn about the views and the motives that made me suppress it for all others.

I

Vincennes

I HAVE SUFFICIENTLY noted, I think, the reasons that compelled me to end all exchanges with Monsieur de Meaux,[2] the trouble that he had in relation to the ideas of fortune that he had formed from them and the dissatisfaction of important people who, having pushed me to this extreme, did not want to have to disavow any of this. It was necessary that I be guilty, that I appear to have been in error. The attestation that Monsieur de Meaux had given me after such a long and rigorous exam did not fit the image that they had wanted to give, either to those who were named my friends or to the public. I was only given the alternative either to go to a convent in the diocese of Meaux, under the direction of this prelate, or to be pushed to all the most awful things that authority and violence could make me envision. The first of these two choices was so repugnant to me, and my depths found themselves so opposed to it, that I did not hesitate for one moment. I let it be known to my friends, who anticipated this and feared what might happen in the future, that I believed that God was asking me never to resume any contact with Monsieur de Meaux, that I was going to look for some place where I could be unknown to the entire human race, and that if God permitted me to succumb to violence, I would consider it as an effect of his will. A few offered me a place to retire, concerning which I sent my regrets to them, not wanting to put anyone in an awkward position in this affair, which had become so abominable and could have drawn them into unfortunate situations.

In the circumstances in which I found myself, I believed that I could only remain safe in the retreat that I had found for myself because, having had some indispensable exchanges with some people on the outside since my return from Meaux, I had reason to fear that someone had some knowledge that might be used to get me arrested. I had looked for another retreat rather far away, but even this contributed to what I wanted to avoid. One of my lady servants, being obligated to go to this house often to move furniture, was recognized by one of the domestic servants of Monsieur Fouquet,[3] who then let others in the area know what I had chosen and soon put Desgrez,[4] charged with arresting me, in a position to know the location of my retreat.

I had hardly lived there for two months when, on one of the feasts of Christmas, Saint John's Day, 1695, I saw a man whom I did not know enter my chamber, who asked me if I was not Madame Guyon. I was in my bed, having been sick for a considerable time; I responded yes to him. And at this he told me that he was arresting me on the orders of the King. I responded to him without emotion that I was ready to obey and to go where he wished. I got up after he had called my maid, and he gave orders that he judged necessary for what remained for him to do. In the street he had surprised another of my maids, who had gone out on some errands. He searched her, and, having found a master key for my house, he used it to enter, accompanied by twenty or thirty people, all armed, whom he distributed where he wanted. After this he went up to my room. This was done with so little sound that neither I nor my other servant heard anything. Desgrez searched everywhere to see if he would not find some papers; there was no nook or cranny that he did not examine. He searched my maid. In the end, he forgot nothing in carrying out his duty and the orders with which he was charged.

He led me to his home first, where he left me alone to go and report what had transpired. I spent one or two nights there while they deliberated about the place where they would lock me up. They finally decided on Vincennes, where I was led with my servants, with the order that I not talk to anyone at all.

A few days later, Monsieur de La Reynie[5] came to interrogate me. His austere air did not frighten me at all. I calmly answered all the questions that he asked of me. He had a truly long list that had been furnished to him with much embellishment; they wanted to make me talk about the people with whom I had been the most connected. I did this in a simple and natural manner without compromising anyone. This interrogation was very long. And although he spoke to me honestly, I noticed that he had been cautioned against me.

He came back a few days later and asked me who had sent the two letters that he showed me, which Desgrez had found in the drawer of a little table that was in my room. I answered him that they were from Father La Combe[6] and that I had received them a few days before being arrested. These two letters were the subject of several interrogations, because they claimed to find some terrible things in them, and Monsieur de La Reynie, who was doing everything in good faith, knowing nothing of the springs that caused this machine to move, took as true all that had been malevolently misconstrued and misinterpreted in these two letters.[7]

There was, however, nothing very helpful in these two letters, which only revolved around piety. At the end of one of these letters, he invited me to go to the waters that were near him. Then, after having testified to the joy that he would have in seeing me, he added that he would not be unhappy to see my family. This word seemed to be something terrible and worthy of the fire. A lot of twists and circumlocutions were necessary for me to understand the ideas that they had formed about this word. And Monsieur de La Reynie used every bit of the skill for catching a criminal to which he could appeal to get from me the knowledge of what he had been made to understand this word could mean. Finally, I started to understand his intention, for until then his terms had been so veiled that I could not imagine how this would end, and I told him: "Sir, you would have saved yourself a lot of pain, and me as well, if you had sought to ask straightaway the explanation of this word, *family*, of which he speaks in this letter; it is the name of the maid who is here. She has served me for twenty years and is very well known by Father La Combe." The prejudice of Monsieur de La Reynie was so great that I had all the trouble in the world to change his mind about this, but finally I gave him such complete proof of it that he needed to give in, which started to open his eyes that the rest of the accusations were hardly better founded.

It said in the same letter that a girl named Jeannette was always in crisis and that she had had very intimate knowledge of me; accordingly, he had sent for me. Concerning this, he wanted to make me tell him what this knowledge was and for what purpose I had been requested. For a long time I refused to respond in a precise manner to the questions that he asked about the above matter, but, finally, having been pushed to the limit, I answered him that I was only refusing to talk about this issue because it was advantageous to me. "But you are being forced to do so," he answered, "and I am ordering you." So I said that this girl had known that I was truly dear to God, that she had said several things of this nature to Father La Combe and that this was why he had sent for me.

There was still one thing in this letter that appeared to have predisposed Monsieur de La Reynie against me in the course of his interrogations. There was a moment when he said, "The Jansenists are at their pinnacle."[8] This made me think that he leaned in that direction, which I had always been quite against. But I only saw righteousness and probity in him.

In the other one of the two letters there was: "The little Church sends you greetings, illustrious persecuted one." It is not possible to express all the torments and pains that I have had to suffer in the course of several interrogations on this expression. They claimed that I wanted to create an independent Church and that it included abominable and mysterious things, of which I alone could reveal the secret. I do not know if Monsieur de La Reynie believed this, but there was nothing that he did not do to get some knowledge of this supposed mystery from me. I told him in vain that this was a simple and natural expression to designate a small number of people united by feeling and charity, as belonging to God in a more particular way than is common for other men, or as Saint Paul expresses it in one of his Epistles, belonging to the same family or the same house—whatever it might be. This term, "little Church," was the subject of a great number of interrogations, the questions of which were, if I am not mistaken, furnished to Monsieur de La Reynie by persons to whom it was important for me to be found guilty. For, as for him, he had too good a mind to be caught up in such minutia.

In the first visits that I received from Monsieur de La Reynie at Vincennes, I told him that there was a very sure way of knowing about my life, and I asked him to request of the King that it be examined. I said that it would be easy to know about it completely and that it would then be rather easy for him to judge thoroughly the things that he claimed to attribute to me. He spoke about this to the King, who found it good. And thus I entered with him into a detailing of all the places where I had been, of all the people who had accompanied me, of those at whose houses I had stayed and with whom I had business—the times, the places, the dates, in which circumstances—including my whole life. He told me, at the end of three months of searching, that nothing had been found against me, that I might remain in my ordinary tranquility. He added, "All justice will be served for you." He undoubtedly believed this would be the case.

Finally, after nine or ten interrogations of six, seven, and sometimes eight hours, he threw the letters and papers on the table with a sort of indignation and said to his clerk in my presence: "Has this person not had enough torment for such little things," as if angry to have caused me so much pain. He requested that they treat me well at Vincennes and made it understood that I would be leaving soon.

He conducted a tenth interrogation, in which he asked my permission to laugh; it was a question of a blue book entitled *Grislidy*[9] that had been found in my home. I told him all the beautiful things about it, and he told me that he would buy it that very evening in order to judge it. After this interrogation he very honestly told me that I had nothing to fear, that everything would be given back to me and that I would be free soon.

I will say that during the whole time I was at Vincennes and Monsieur de La Reynie was interrogating me, I remained in great peace, very happy to spend all my life in prison. There was so little daylight in the place where they put me that I hardly saw it at all. Finally, it was necessary to put me near the spot where light came in, so as to do more work.

[3.20.5][10] I used to compose hymns, which the girl who served me was learning by heart as I was composing them, so as to be able to retain them, and we were singing your praises, O my God. I considered myself like a little bird that you held in a cage for your pleasure, which must sing in order to fulfill her condition in life. The stones of my tower seemed like rubies to me, meaning that I esteemed them more than all of the magnificent things of the century. My joy was founded on your love, O my God, and on the pleasure of being your captive. Although I only had these reflections while composing these hymns, the bottom of my heart was full of that joy that you give to those who love you in the midst of the greatest difficulties.

[3.20.6] This peace was altered for a few moments by an infidelity that I committed. This was to premeditate, one day, the responses that I should make during an interrogation that I was supposed to undergo the next day.[11] I responded to everything with difficulty, and God, so faithful in my regard, who had made me respond to difficult and confused things with much ease and presence of mind, knew well how to punish me for my forethought. He hardly let me answer very easy things and permitted me to remain almost without knowing what to say. One infidelity that I committed, I say, altered my peace for a few days, but it came back soon, and I believe, my Lord, that you only permitted this fault to show the uselessness of our plans in such meetings, and the sureness of trusting in you. Those who still ground themselves on human reason will say that it is necessary to prepare and arrange, that to act otherwise is to tempt God and to wait for miracles. I let others think what they want. As for me, I only find security in abandoning myself to the Lord. All scripture is full of witnesses who ask for this abandonment. *Commit your way to the hands of the Lord and he will act himself* (Ps. 37:5). *Abandon yourself to his guidance and he will lead your steps himself.*[12] God has not meant to set traps for us in telling us this and in teaching us to not premeditate our responses.

The testimony of Monsieur de La Reynie, decided on my innocence, only served to embitter the people who persecuted me. Not only did they not free me, but they also did not let either Monsieur de La Reynie or even Desgrez come to see me. For the latter esteemed Monsieur de La Reynie as much as he had once had preconceived notions against me. In place of Monsieur de La Reynie, they sent me Monsieur Pirot.[13] Desgrez, having learned that they no longer wanted him to see me because they were getting rid of him, assured them that he was very opposed to me and appeared to believe all that they were saying. Then he came back and told me that Monsieur de La Reynie had told him: "Let's get out of this; they want me to make this woman guilty, and

I find her very innocent. I do not want to serve as an instrument of her downfall." As might be expected, he was given another assignment, and I have never seen him since. The one who came after him acted very differently.

A little later they sent me Monsieur Pirot, who spoke to me with great sourness and anger. He wanted once more to go over the interrogations that had been conducted with me at Saint Marie's by Monsieur l'Official[14] in his presence, eight or nine years before. And since these interrogations were truly to my benefit, through the assistance of my Divine Master, he wanted to rewrite them to make them very negative. After having tormented me to the point of making me sick, for there was nothing more violent than what they did to me, he wanted me to tell him all the bad things imaginable about Father La Combe. He had never been able to pardon him for what this Father had once said in the presence of Monsieur l'Official: "You are a doctor in Israel, and you do not know these things!"[15] I responded that I had only good things to say about him and that I would not have confessed to him so long ago if I had noticed the least thing. He got angry about that, to the point that he was no longer balanced. I have never known a more bitter or tyrannical man. He wanted me to give him a declaration that I would no longer let myself be directed by this Father and that I would have no more dealings with him. I accepted his terms a little—although I might recognize that Father La Combe was a holy man, I consented never to let myself be directed by him, since Monsignor the Archbishop did not deem this acceptable, and to have no dealings with him in the future, preferring obedience to all the rest.

A little while later, he came back to tell me that he was unhappy with what I had put in this declaration—that it was out of obedience that I would have no further dealings with this Father. They wanted me to put that it was because he was a dangerous, heretical man whose dealings were very bad, and, finally, a man whose memory must be wiped out with horror. I responded: "Sir, the Father is a saint and a man with an irreproachable life, in whom I have only ever seen goodness. That would be to speak against my conscience and to commit a great sin." He then told me: "This is what they want of you, without which you will never participate in the sacraments." I told him concerning this: "It never pleases God to procure the sacraments by a crime, and although I desire extremely to receive our Lord, whom I love uniquely, I prefer to be deprived of it all my life than to buy it with a crime as black as a testimony against my conscience would be."

He then made me understand, with pretended gentleness, that I should not expose myself through my resistance to the unpleasant consequences that this resistance could cause me, but in order to cut through these pleas, I told him: "Sir, although I suffer here all that one can suffer, such as to cause the continuous pains with which I have been so long overwhelmed, through the bad treatment that it has become their mission to make me endure, I declare to you that I prefer to stay here all my life than to leave here this way, and that nothing in the world is capable of weakening me." It is true that the torments that this man caused me through his ruses and artifices made me fall ill every time that he came, but this was hardly painful. Finally, I became extremely sick. I had a continual loss of consciousness with a high fever.

The commandant, very devoted to the people who persecuted me, was, without ceasing, preoccupied with trying to trick me and to surprise me with his words, with a view toward gaining favor with them this way. He treated me in the harshest ways, refusing me certain little sources of relief that were given to prisoners and the most criminal. This was done to make his fortune by oppressing me. He claimed that I was hardly sick, in order to make me miss out on the most necessary things.

In this extremity I asked for a confessor in order to die a Christian. I was asked who I would like. I called for Father Archange Enguerrand,[16] a reformed Franciscan of great merit, or else a Jesuit. Not only did they not want to let anyone come, but they made it seem like this request was criminal. They were no longer reasonable with me, and they verbally insulted me at a time when I was hardly able to hear them. They let a doctor come see me after a great crisis that I had, and only God knows all that I suffered from these attacks that I found coming at me from all sides at that time. Monsieur Pirot, offended that I had asked for another confessor, no longer wanted to come, which pleased me greatly, but he became strangely enraged against me.

I hoped that I would no longer see anyone. And I was happy, O my God, to stay there for the rest of my life. My solitude was my delight. I composed verses and hymns when I was so moved. We sang, and we spent our retreat in a delicious manner in spite of all the bodily pains, the discomfort of prison and the strictness of our guards. What was most painful in this place was that they would only come twice during the day, however sick one might be, with no help at night. There was one time when my chambermaid thought me nearly dead for four hours. She cried, called out, and got very distressed, but in vain; no help came. As for me, since I am very persuaded that it is not men for whom I must wait in extreme situations, this did not cause me any pain, but the fright that this poor girl had when she thought she saw me die without help and had to spend the night alone with a corpse was an intolerable torment.

Toward the end of the time that I spent at Vincennes, they proposed to have me see the parish priest at Saint-Sulpice.[17] He had not been long in Paris before he occupied a considerable place. I did not know him at all, but I believed that, since he had connections with one of the men whom I held in the highest esteem, who was Monsieur Tronson,[18] I would find in him what I could have found in the other. I felt some repugnance, however, toward the first proposition that was made to me, but since it was proposed in such a way as to let me know that they wanted the thing, it was necessary for me to suffer through what I could not prevent.

He came to me then, and, falling to his knees as soon as he had entered my chamber, he spent a quarter of an hour in prayer without speaking a single word to me. This beginning and this pretentiousness made a certain impression of fear on me that was only proven true later on. He told me that he came on behalf of Monsieur Tronson, who took great interest in all that concerned me, that he was a close friend of this priest and his family, that he wanted to be of service to me, that he did not know why they had sent me Monsieur Pirot, who was a very hard man, that he had examined the *Short and Easy Method*, that he had found it very good, and that he was going to express his view to Monsieur Pirot. All these reasons and the apparent simplicity that he pretended to have, the outer signs of piety, won me over and got me to answer him with much frankness. But, my God, who knows the depths of hearts, you know how different his words were from his actions! His first visit happened in this way. I dreamed of several things that should have made me wary of him if I had only stopped to think about them. And I believe that they were warnings from the Lord rather than dreams. His laugh had something forced in it, and what he said to my chambermaid started to open my eyes.

Since he knew that she was very attached to me, he tried to get her to oppose me, promised her a better condition, and appeared touched by her difficulty in a place such as this one. "My leaving Madam, sir? There is no other situation in Paris that I might want; Madam is more to me than all of that!" I do not know whether, in what I report about others, I use their same terms, but the meaning is the same. I scolded her for her answer when she told it to me, and I told her that he would not stop there and that if he returned to that request, she must tell him that it should not appear that she would leave me where I was, but when I was released from there and in a situation where I did not need her, she would reflect on the goodness that he had shown her, but it would be against her honor to abandon me now. He appeared content with this last response, which she made to him when he spoke to her about it again, and expressed no doubt that he would follow through with it.

Some time later, he asked me for my signature, which was what I feared the most because of the surprises that they could create for me with it. He did not fail, when he came to see me, to get on his knees in my chamber. Pretensions must be considered suspicious, and I have much experience with them. He told me that he would bring me something that I must sign in a few days, which consisted of professions of faith, submissions. I told him: "Sir, since I cannot sign without knowing what I am signing, and I have been tormented until now for using vague terms and not knowing the meaning of the terms, I ask that you would show what they want me to sign to Monsieur Tronson, that he draw it up, and that he sign it, and I will blindly sign what comes from his hand." This proposition seemed to trouble him, and he told me to think hard about it.

It is important to understand that they had had the priest come because Monsieur Tronson had shown kindness toward me. And they were reassured that a person not suspected by Tronson would not give bad impressions of them to him. Moreover, this priest was a friend of the Bishop of Ch[artres] who had also readily accepted the bad things that had been said about me, and they could not have done this more effectively than through a man who must have seemed to him completely disinterested. This succeeded just as they had planned.

He came back two days afterwards and told me: "You are wrong to have asked for Monsieur Tronson and only to want to sign what he proposes to you. He will treat you more strictly than I would have, and this would have been a better deal for you." I answered him that since I had said this, I would remain firm. He came back more than two months later for two or three days: one, to tell me that I was losing by letting myself deal with Monsieur Tronson, and, then, that it would be impossible for me to sign what he was bringing me on his behalf. I stayed firm on this and never wanted to abandon it.

Finally, seeing that I would not change my mind, he brought up a letter that I wrote to Monsieur Tronson, in which I revealed the pain caused me by all of these signatures that they did not cease to demand of me. For, not knowing the meaning of the terms, I feared to imply something that might be inferred as my having sentiments contrary to faith. And I begged him to draw up a submission for me himself that might be able to satisfy Monsieur de Paris[19] and to protect me from the impressions that they were endeavoring to give the public against me.

Monsieur Tronson sent me one fully composed and written by his hand and assured me that it appeared to him that I could sign it in all confidence that it contained nothing that might be able to do the least possible harm to holy doctrine or to solid truths about interior ways. It said that one would be happy with the condemnation of my books whose expressions could be taken the wrong way, excusing myself for the rest and justifying myself concerning the meaning of terms contrary to my intentions. This was, in effect, what I had requested.

The parish priest, while bringing me Monsieur Tronson's response, put this submission in my hands. It held essentially that I had never strayed from the sentiments of the Catholic Church, my mother, for whom I always had, have now and, by the grace of God, will have all my life all possible commitment, and that if my ignorance had made me use less precise terms, my feelings have always been righteous, etc. For, in the end, whatever persecution might have been leveled against me, everything has always revolved around these terms. I signed the paper as they brought it to me.

The parish priest got on his knees in his usual way and told me that he was more enlightened by me than if he had seen me perform miracles. Then he told me that I would have my freedom soon. This was the thing in the world to which I was the most indifferent. For, by my choice, I would have preferred to be in this place where nothing could be falsely attributed to me, whatever discomfort I might feel, than to have my freedom in order to feel new suspicions every day and to be the subject of new tragedies. My solitude was so sweet, having a girl with me from whom I hid nothing and with whom I could pray and stay silent when it pleased me, that, without the perpetual interrogations that I had to suffer, I would have preferred prison to all the delights of life because my pleasure cannot be in these things, but in God. The ability to find him without being subjected to seeing or speaking to creatures was luxurious to me.

The next day after all that, the priest, who had been so satisfied with my submission the day before, came to see me with a severe air, like a school teacher. He told me that they were convinced that all that I had signed was mere hypocrisy, that they no longer esteemed me and that they were not happy. I said to him that this was all I could do and that they could therefore only leave me there. I would be happy to finish out my days there.

But God was not yet content with what I had suffered, nor were my enemies—which comes to the same thing because I could only look at them as instruments of the hand of God—nor were my enemies, I say, with what they had made me suffer. Since I had not heard mass on Easter day or since I had been there, they used this desire that I had to fulfill this duty and to receive my sacraments to torment me once more. A chapel near my tower was blessed. Then they came to tell me that I would not receive the sacraments unless I signed a statement that I would not have any director other than Monsieur de Paris and that he would have the care of my soul. Far from feeling repugnance, I had much joy, and I flattered myself that Monsieur de Paris, by getting to know me profoundly himself, would have feelings toward me that were more balanced than those which others had inspired in him. But it did not happen like this because, from that time, he never investigated, at least with me, whether I had a reasonable and Christian soul. On the contrary, he treated me as if my soul, like that of a beast, would die with my body. Whether or not I served and loved God was of little consequence provided that my reputation was not blackened in the eyes of men.

Sometime later the parish priest, who no longer performed his prayers, came back, but with an air full of anger. He told me that Monsieur de Paris was not happy with what I had signed from Monsieur Tronson, that he was offended and that it was necessary to sign another submission, without which the sacraments would not be given to me. I asked what fault there was with Monsieur Tronson's statement. He responded that it was because it was signed by him, and that they only wanted the same, but I should have written it by my hand and signed it. I said that this would not be difficult and that if they brought me the one by Monsieur Tronson, I would transcribe it and sign it. They came back a bit later and brought me one all prepared that they said was transcribed from that of Monsieur Tronson. I did not want to sign it without seeing his, but they never wanted to show it to me.

I swear that nothing in the world ever made me suffer as much as these signatures. For since I do not know the meaning of the terms, and all the torments that were carried out upon me were only about these terms, I was always afraid that someone would sneak something in there that I did not believe, and I would have preferred to die. I saw so many intelligent people occupied in trying to surprise me and trick me, and me, being without counsel, alone, without education. The reason for this is that M. de Meaux had already made me sign one of these submissions, which I would sign again since it was on the same subject as M. Tronson's and said nearly the same thing, but Monsieur de Paris wanted to have his own.

Finally, I asked at least to read it. They read it to me without giving it to me. But since I was apprehensive about surprises and they did not want me to read it, neither did I want to sign it. They brought me another one a bit later, or the same one, which I did read. I found nothing there that spoke about the same thing as the others, at least as far as I can judge in my ignorance and with the pain that I felt. They held a sword to my back every day. They asked me for letters for Monsieur de Paris, which they brought to me fully composed, which it was necessary to copy, and this in order to have the chance to torment me.

It is something that must surprise everyone that, with Monsieur de Meaux always treating me as an ignorant woman who knew nothing at all, they treated me with more rigor than the most skilled theologian who had committed voluntary errors on the most essential points of our faith.

Exactly as I said before the condemnation of my books, when bad books are written, one is content to condemn them without tormenting the people, unless they write in support of the condemned books. And, further, how should they be treated? At most, they are exiled. But I who have only erred concerning a few terms, according to Monsieur de Meaux himself, which do not relate to theology in the strict sense, with my not being a theologian, and only concern the matter of contemplative prayer, about which others than I have written more strongly, why should I be put in prison, I who have always submitted with all my heart? Why torment me for nearly twenty years for the same thing, when, even without requiring so many submissions and admissions of error from me, I might have abjured to protest my commitment to the church? I had always asked that my books be condemned if they were found bad and that at least I might be left in peace. I have never been able to obtain this.

I said many times to the parish priest: "Sir, if I am thinking badly, let me be put right; if I am praying badly, let me be told how they want me to do this, because I have neither attachment nor will." He responded that my contemplative prayer was good and that there was nothing to change there. I responded to him: "But if it is good, why do you torment me?"—no response at all. O my God, it is true that I am a prodigy of your mercies and my own wretchedness, because what greater mercy is there than to be called to conform to the image of your Son?

I had forgotten to say that, while putting me in Vincennes, they confiscated my little Jesus of wax and my image of Saint Michael, or at least kept them for a long time with the authorities. They asked me, where did this devotion to the child Jesus come from; what did "Little Jesus" mean? They did the same thing to me in several interrogations, and also about my devotion to Saint Michael. Such bad things had been said about me, and they believed these so firmly, that they thought that I honored Saint Michael because the Devil was in the image. And they told me, without spelling it out, without daring to say it openly, that it was the Devil that I adored. This thought makes me shudder with horror.

In order to return to my story, finally, after much trouble, the parish priest came to hear my confession. Mass was said, and he gave me communion. I took communion thus on Sundays and feast days. They would have wanted to leave me at Vincennes, and I would have really wanted to stay there, too, but they did not dare to leave me because Monsieur de La Reynie knew the truth. The parish priest suggested a strategy to get me out, but in such a manner that they would always be the masters of my fate and they would dispose of my person according to what was agreeable to the interests of someone or other.

For this, he made a girl come from Lower Brittany, where she was in a kind of community that until then had not been able to obtain an establishment in Paris, although it had been requesting this for a long time. He believed he could not have found a more favorable arrangement to get them here than to propose to put me with the girls, for whom he was the superior. It is a kind of Congregation of Saint Augustine. There are one, two or three sisters in each house. They built this community right away for these girls in Vaugirard. One sister was placed there with a peasant who was taken to be her servant. I was put into this community, constructed in haste, when I was made to leave Vincennes. But they had taken every precaution beforehand to be assured of her and her devotion, either to mistreat me or to make sure that all the people involved were in agreement with their plans.

The parish priest came to tell me with a gracious air that he was going to bring me back to my home; I let all be said and done. He had proposed before to have me put in the general hospital! God knows that, loving the poor and humiliation, I would not have had any problem with this, but they did not dare, due to my family. He spoke of sending me to Bourges. I said that I preferred Vincennes. His plan, as the following events will show, was to have me escape on the way and to say that my friends had absconded with me, because they wanted to implicate them in my downfall. Finally, he came to swear that he was going to bring me back to my home, and that first I would be taken to Monsieur Tronson's home. He said this so that I would not be surprised to find myself outside of Paris.

2

Vaugirard

ON OCTOBER 16, 1696, Desgrez came to take me from Vincennes in order to bring me to Vaugirard. As soon as I saw this, I suspected that they had tricked me, because when one wants to bring you back to your home, one simply frees you, and one does not use a minister of the people. I told him that I clearly saw that I had been tricked and that I was going to be brought to some place where they would be in charge, in order to force me to make the false allegations that they wanted. I asked insistently to stay at Vincennes, but they did not want this. I could not prevent myself from shedding some tears, and Monsieur de Bernaville[1] told me that it was truly astonishing that, not having cried upon arriving, I would cry while leaving! I told him that, in these places, someone was witness to my conduct, but that in another place without witnesses, it would be easy to say whatever they wanted about my conduct to the public. This was the reason that they did not want to put me in a convent; there are too many witnesses, and not everyone would damn me through false allegations such as those that they wanted to make up about me. This was why, I was told, they would never put me there, and because I was winning everyone over in such a way that they only would say good things about me. I was therefore taken to Vaugirard.

When I saw that there was only one girl, I truly understood their intention better. I said this to the parish priest, who assured me by his place in heaven that I was mistaken and that within three months I would be taken to my home. However, they forgot nothing at all in getting this girl to do her duty well. They promised to make her General Superior of her congregation, although she had never had a job and the others could never live with her. But, provided that something was said or done against me, they would not forget to reward it. The parish priest, who normally gave her room and board, instead put the money into her hands and prohibited her to give me a cent, but told her to give me what I needed generously and to write it down. They began by making me buy game, which I do not eat at all, and many other things, so as to make people think that I lived extravagantly, and to be able to use that later to decry me and make me out to be a sensual person. When I asked them to buy me meat from the butcher that I like a lot, they could not get it, and they made me buy so many chickens that, not being able to eat them, I let them become hens, of which there remain a great quantity, as well as young chicks. I bought everything at a high price.

I was put in a cloister room that was ready to collapse. While I was there, it was necessary to rebuild the foundation because, in order to spare the pillars, everything was supported by a dangerous pole. I thought I was going to break a leg while walking on the floor. I did not say one word, although I saw myself at any moment being buried under the ruins of this building. I kept to the garden as much as I could; they made this a crime, as I will explain later.

When I was in this house, they let the doors remain open at first, and they started a rumor that my friends wanted to break me out. I saw the malevolence of this conduct at once, and I easily understood that they had some designs to have me kidnapped and to blame it on my friends and my family. They would surely have put me in a place where no one would ever know what had become of me. I told the girl who guarded me that if someone came to kidnap me, I would cry out so loudly that everyone would hear it. For neither my friends nor my children would ever do this, but they wanted to kidnap me to cause the downfall of others.

I wrote to Monsieur Tronson, a righteous and admirable man who judged others for himself. He communicated to me that he had seen Monsieur de Paris and N. and that, after having heard them speak on the subject about which I was suspicious, he could assure me that they had no particular designs on me that might have the least relation to what I feared, and that in my regard they only had thoughts of moderation and peace. He thought it was this way.

But immediately after the parish priest saw that he had missed his chance, they locked me up, they blocked the window on the side of the kitchen garden, they plugged all the holes in the garden wall, down to the smallest one at the top of the wall, and they made the wall higher. From this moment on, they no longer held anything back concerning me. I still had a little porch that opened up onto two little rooms. They forbade me to go through the door. I had nothing at all except my chamber and a passage to enter it. Since the fireplace had been demolished, it was necessary, with whatever heat there might be, that I cook in my room. This room, whose ceiling was very low, being exposed all day to the sun and having a little window that they had blocked but gave some air, was uninhabitable. I used to go into the open air in the garden, although it was still hot. I would seek out shady places.

They accused me of having men pass over the walls through Monsieur de La Reynie's garden. The gardener assured them in vain that the door of the house was always closed, that no one entered and that he had never seen anyone on top of their walls. They wanted to say this, although they knew that the opposite was true.

This girl who guarded me, as I said, had been warned in such an outlandish way about me that she looked at me like a devil. All the straightforward things that I did for her only offended her. She believed that these were done with a view toward winning her over. Since she got bored in this little house, where she was all alone, and she looked at me as the cause of the assiduity that they were requiring of her, she treated me in an offensive way at every moment, saying that she was only pretending to be bothered by me for love of me, adding vulgarities that were hard to hear.

Monsieur de Paris showed much satisfaction in the way that she conducted herself with regard to me and told her that she had more courage and illumination than all the nuns who had guarded me before in not letting herself be tricked and won over.

Often she would come and insult me, telling me rude things, putting her fist under my chin, so as to make me angry. She treated me like the vilest person so as to be able to claim that I had said or done something which they could claim was a crime. But God helped me infinitely, because I am quick-witted and animated, and patience, by the grace of God, was never lacking.

One night a frightening wind was blowing that downed and uprooted trees in all the gardens. They found a downed apricot tree in theirs. She said it was me who had downed it. She sent for men to use them as witnesses that I had cracked this tree. In my room I heard a gardener say that four strong men would obviously not be able to knock down this tree as neatly as this and that it had been the wind. This man added that five or six of his apricot trees in the full wind, like this one here, had been downed in his garden. This did not stop them from putting this among my crimes.

Since I only had one fireplace, on the day of fasting she had masons come around dinner time. The workers said that it was necessary to put out the fire. She came to put out the fire before me, believing that I would be opposed to it and that some words that would show my impatience would escape from me, such as might be used against me. I did not say one word and went into the garden, happy not to dine. I noticed in the garden a walled, hollowed-out door, with stones above it. I told my girls, who could not tolerate this without pain, to say nothing and to cook some eggs. This place was far from the house, and we used it in this way in order to avoid giving to this girl a reason to make some bad report about me. But not having been able to get me angry, she devised a way to do even better for herself by accusing me of having wanted to burn down the house. Every day there were new accusations.

The parish priest said the most offensive things in the world to me outside of the confessional, to the point of making me understand that he suspected that I was a witch. But when he heard my confession, he told me that he found me very innocent, that he considered all this to be a trial from God. Outside of that, he said that he was always furious with me. This difference between the priest who acts as a minister and holds the place of God and the fanatical man is truly remarkable. Also, I have never cast him off, and I can say what it is to confess without difficulty to one's greatest enemies. It was you alone, Lord, to whom I confessed myself, and I exposed my naked soul before your divine eyes.

He tried to explain to me that he wanted me to see the newspaper. I rejected this as much as I could due to the trouble of sending for it and my lack of time to read it. He wanted this. At once, he sent me the *Mercure Galant*.[2] I knew where all of this was going. I did not want any more of it. He took communion away from me because of my disobedience. He asked me if I wanted a blue bird that my daughter had sent me, which was at his home. I believed that it really was a bird, and, since I like them, I asked him to send it to me. It was a little book of fairy tales. This was added to the rest of my crimes. He said that I threw letters over the walls.

I had terrible dreams about him; sometimes I would see him vomit a black substance on me, and at other times it seemed to me that our Lord made him take off his clothes and clothed him in another, dirty way.

He came to tell me once that if Monsieur de Cambrai[3] had not written his book, I would have my freedom. At other times he said that the book was against me. I never heard him say a true word or the same thing twice; he was always confused, often speaking through his teeth like a man who threatens and who does not want to speak clearly about things. Sometimes he wanted to know in whose hands I had put the discharge paper from Monsieur de Meaux in order to try to get it back;[4] sometimes he had me understand that they had no interest in my submission.

In the beginning, when I saw him, I gave him a letter for Monsieur Tronson, full of confidential information. He swore to me, on his faith as a priest, that he would give it to him without anyone seeing it. He brought it to Monsieur de Paris, who was angry with me about it; then, while talking to me, he cut it up and, finally, made me understand that he had shown it to him.

The more I confided in him at the beginning, the tighter my heart became, and I believed that this confidence was harming me. I spoke willingly and with simplicity concerning my faults and my miseries. I would sometimes say: "O my God, if you want me once more to be a spectacle *to men and to angels* (1 Cor. 4:9), may your holy will be done. All I ask is that you save those who are yours and not permit them to be separated from you. *Never let the powers, the principalities, the sword, etc., separate us from the charity of God which is in Jesus Christ* (Rom. 8:38-39). As for my particular situation, what does it matter to me what men think of me; what does it matter what they make me suffer, since they cannot separate me from Jesus Christ, who is engraved at the bottom of my heart. If I displease Jesus Christ, though I might please all men, it would make me less than mud. Let all men therefore scorn me and hate me, provided that I am agreeable to him. Their blows will polish what is defective in me so that I may be presented to the one for whom I die every day, until he comes to consummate this death." And I would pray to you, O my God, to make me an offering pure and clean in your blood, so as to be offered to you.[5]

Around the month of March in the year 1697, I had the impression that the King was dying and would not live through the month of September.[6] I said this to the parish priest with my ordinary simplicity, and I asked him to tell it to one or two of the people who knew my friends, whom I believed it important to inform. A few days later, it entered my mind that God may have permitted this impression in order to disparage me in the mind of the priest. I was not troubled about this, and I found myself ready for all of the humiliation and confusion that he would not fail to make me suffer, with the preconceived notions that he had against me, if it happened that I was mistaken. God knows how much this faithfulness still costs people still living in themselves and what agonies nature suffers before reaching a kind of death, the completion of which God requires of souls who want to be entirely his. If such things happened today and I had a similar impulse, I would say the same thing. But the parish priest was far from understanding this simplicity. When I would make some efforts to trust him with some confidences, I felt that he did not entertain what I was telling him, and that most often he did not understand for lack of intelligence. And my heart had no correspondence there.

I had three little crosses in the garden, and I had written there: "I go from cross to cross, and thus spend my life." They even made that a crime. I observed Lent with guns blazing,[7] although I was very sick, even before starting it. But I had the impulse to do this, though it might cost me my life. Although rather poorly nourished and lacking provisions, and although I had not been free from fever since the Sunday before Lent, not only did they not suggest that I break with Lent, but I also fasted entirely, although with very sore eyes and a sore throat, which, added to the fever, the coughing and a violent head-ache, might have made them believe that I needed some other nourishment. But I did not sense that this was God's will. I would have been more open to this due to the order that was given at the time to this girl not to have a single priest come to me, even at death, if this same will of God had not been prefer-able to me over all things.

There were moments when the parish priest seemed to have some compas-sion for my state. He would speak to me with some gentleness, but whether it was from inconsistency or weakness in relation to the people who were inter-ested in my downfall, it would not last long. He made a thousand proposals to me, each more painful than the next, and vowed certain things with hor-rible sermons. Later, it was completely the opposite. What afflicted me some-times to excess was being obligated to confess to a man who oppresses you and declares himself the cruelest of your enemies. Sometimes I would be treated as if I were scandalous, hypocritical and a witch, sometimes as if I had commit-ted crimes in Brittany, where I had never been, on which they nonetheless insisted to my face. He would exhort me to declare my spells. The stinging taunts that he directed at me concerning people about whom I cared afflicted me more than the rest. He pretended to hear my confession, without letting me take communion, in order to give the impression that he acted knowingly. It was sometimes an intolerable pain for me to be obligated to confess to him. And I found that it was a kind of impiety to obligate me to do this without his believing anything that I said to him. I swear that this was one of the things about which I was the most sensitive.

He summoned a man to come with him one day with the parents of one of the two girls who were serving me, with the intention of taking her from me, but she made such loud cries that they did not dare to execute their plan in broad daylight. This sister who guarded me was in on the plot and had sepa-rated her flawlessly from the company of the other girl, for fear that she might be of help to her. He has asked her since then to leave me, but the poor girl was far from doing so.

A few days later, this sister came into my chamber to block up the only window from which I had any air. I found myself reduced to one single room, where it was necessary to do the cooking, wash the dishes and the rest. My girl, who found herself alone there because I had gone down to the garden, told her that she would not tolerate their suffocating me in my room and that, not finding me there, she could not permit them to block the window. So the sister, with the fury of a lion, came to find me in the garden. I rose to greet her. She told me what had just happened. I responded, with as much honesty that

I could, that when the parish priest came, I would blindly do all that he ordered, and that this was what he had recommended. She cried out, like a fish
monger, holding one hand on her head and the other out to my chin, that she
knew me well, that she knew who I was and what I was capable of doing, that
she was well informed and that I did not believe her to be as knowledgeable as
she was—all of this together with gestures full of menace and violence. I told
her with gentleness that I was known by people of honor. "How," she answered, "do you say that I am not a person of honor?"—and that in terrible
anger. I responded to her without raising my voice: "I say, Mademoiselle, that
I am known by persons of honor, and I will report your actions to the parish
priest." "I do not recommend that," she told me—"you would find yourself in
a bad way, and I know what I will do." This was a disturbance that went on for
a very long time, during which she said the most offensive things to me to hurt
me and to make me say something to her of the same nature, but my God did
not permit it. It is necessary to undergo this sort of treatment continuously to
understand how it irritates one's nature and makes it suffer, although it is not
permitted one word to unburden itself. I had always treated this girl honestly,
giving her all that I believed myself capable of giving to please her. I do not
know if she was not being pushed to these things so that I might be taken
away from there and locked up in an unknown place, or to make me complain
and get angry or ask for another thing. But the One for whom I suffered gave
me patience and did not permit me to let the least complaint escape. I did not
speak to the parish priest about what had happened, and I abandoned everything to God. But having found out that one of the workers present at this
scene had said that there must be some women of ill repute locked up in this
house, I asked the parish priest to come to see me. I told him that it was truly
enough to be locked up like I was, without having to hear such atrocious insults and to suffer treatments of this nature, and that, if I was guilty, then let
me have a trial, but that it was abominable to expose me to such infamies.

He appeared to be angry and left to go issue a reprimand, according to
what he told me, and to forbid her from using these insults this way in the
future. He came back and reproached me greatly for not having confidence in
him. He said that he had been assured that one of my important friends had
come to see me, that a lot had been repeated about how Monsieur de Paris
had made me leave Vincennes. He said that all my friends had abandoned me,
and that, having no more protectors, I must expect the worst. I answered him
that he knew better than anyone that I could not see the person of whom he
spoke, being in a situation as hidden from view as mine was. As for Vincennes,
I said that I was ready to return there if they wanted, that I was no less locked

up in the place where I now found myself, that at least I would be shielded from these supposed visits about which he was speaking to me, and that I asked for no grace, being resolved to suffer all for God.

After every fury that seized him, he would soften up and tell me that he wanted to be of service to me, but that he was obligated to speak ill of me sometimes, that Monsieur de Meaux, while introducing him, had said: "That is really a man there! One cannot put her in better hands." He assured me that he would protect me against the storm and that he would smooth everything out, but that he desired testimony from me that he had charity and that I had reason to praise him. He played all sorts of characters and finally instructed me to write him a beautiful letter thanking him, which I did.

The trouble from this sister of whom I have spoken derived from the fact that another sister of the same congregation, who had come to spend a short time in the house at the beginning, and toward whom she felt hatred and horrible jealousy, seemed to have liked me and spoke well of me at every occasion. This girl would sometimes speak candidly with me about the other sisters in Paris, who seemed to me very angry about the way that this one acted. They told me that her temperament was such that no one could live with her, and they beseeched me not to let myself become too troubled by what she could do to me.

They blocked up yet another door, and as for the window that had caused such a fuss, they were happy to mount a wooden trellis over it. They locked me up at my own expense, and they paid for the chains and the walls that held me captive with my money.

A bit later, the parish priest came to see me to forbid my communicating with Monsieur de Paris. And taking on a very serious air, he told me that Maillard[8] had come to see him and had told him some things so forcefully that there was no way not to believe her. He added that I was responsible before God for all the troubles of the Church, that I had corrupted this and that person, and that I must feel such great remorse of conscience. Then, he urged me to examine my conscience, to be converted and not to be damned.

I told him: "But, sir, after having given everything up as I have done, and having given myself to God...." He interrupted me without wanting to let me finish, telling me that he had known witches who had done things for the Devil greater than what the saints had done for God, but that they had converted and had died well. He urged me to take advantage of his charity toward me and said that he held out his hands, and that I should take advantage of this time. He said that he did not doubt at all that Father La Combe was a second Louis Goffridy,[9] who was burned at Marseilles, and that, if I sent him away, he would believe the same of me. He said, finally, that they were providing me with a grace by letting me suffer in the place where I was. I responded to him that if they found that it was necessary for me to go to another prison, that I was ready to go there.

Concerning what I told him about Maillard being a bad woman, etc., he answered me that thieves would often accuse each other and could not be believed.

For most of the visits that he made to me, his discourse was of this nature, and you gave me the grace, O my God, to suffer everything for your love. When I sometimes spoke to tell him the truth or to enlighten him, although I did it as sweetly as was possible for me, he told me that I was an angry person, and that if I had virtue I would not make any reply. And then he would begin exhorting me to take advantage of the opportunity I had and to confess my crimes to him. My unique consolation, O my God, is that you see the bottom of our hearts. Whether it is that you wanted to punish me for displeasing you without knowing it, or you wanted to use me, it is always a result of your kindness.

During a visit that he paid me later, he told me that the reason communion had been taken away from me was that to let me be seen taking communion would justify me too much and would cause them to be judged for their ill treatment of me.

He told me again that trustworthy people had told him that I was preaching from the tops of the walls. No one was in a better position to disabuse them of this notion than he was, if he had wanted, given the care with which I was guarded in this house and the excessive exhaustion of my body, which had made me unable to stir or support myself without help for years.

Sometime afterwards he came back to torment me excessively in order to make me confess lies, and he told me that I was delusional and that a person who is delusional is capable of anything. I answered him that, as for being delusional, I might be so in good faith, but that it was necessary to let me know in what way I was mistaken and this was all that I wanted. I said that he might remember that I had told him I would try to perform contemplative prayer as I was ordered, but that nothing about that had been prescribed. I said that I would, therefore, remain in my good faith until I was told otherwise, and that concerning matters of fact, neither prison, nor questions, nor death would make me confess falsehoods, but that I would say no more to justify myself. He then said the harshest things to me.

What often caused me great pain was the torment that he inflicted on my girls to make them confess the falsest things. If they said: "This is not true," they were angry. If they did not say anything, they were considered convinced. He had developed a terrible aversion toward one of them. And when she wanted to defend me against some claim that was neither true nor reasonable, he told her that this in itself showed her to have a wicked soul and that he judged her to have all sorts of vices. And above all that, he refused her absolution.

I dreamed during that time that I wanted to pass through a door so narrow that it was almost impossible to do so. N.[10] told me to pass through it, and I made efforts that seemed to be about to crush me. He held out his hand; I passed through with a lot of pain. I believed myself, while passing, to have caused the door to fall on him, and I remained very frightened. But with one hand he replaced it, and I found myself with him in a very spacious church, full of very many people. Since I was outside, I found that everyone was eating the leaves of green oak trees, and no one offered me any. I did not want any of these, explaining that I ate more solid meat. They reproached me for my bad taste, saying that this was most in fashion and that everyone found them excellent. It is only too true that one makes meals of leaves and rejects the living and life-giving bread.

I dreamed another time of my sister, the nun who was dead, telling me: "Get out! Even if you were only living in caves and quarries, surviving on the bread obtained by begging, you would be happier." My heart was prepared to do all that it pleased God to command, too happy to give blood for blood, life for life.

3

Missing Evidence

A LITTLE LATER the parish priest, having come to see me, told me that Monsieur de Paris had some incontestable evidence of crimes that I had committed, and that as such he did not see that they would ever grant me my freedom.

I told him that I was not asking for it and had never asked for it, but I found it very strange, after having spent ten months at Vincennes in the hands of Monsieur de La Reynie, a man strongly informed and warned about me at first, and after so many interrogations, that these supposed crimes should still be discussed with me. I said that from the beginning of my difficulties I had asked for my life to be examined, that I had addressed myself to Monsieur de Meaux and to others, offering to put myself in whatever prison they wanted during the interrogation they would undertake. I said that this was even the first thing that I had asked Monsieur de La Reynie the first time that he came to interrogate me and that, having requested him to ask the King on my behalf that this examination be conducted, the King told him that my request was reasonable, and afterwards Monsieur de La Reynie had documented all the places I had been, all the people who had accompanied me, those who lodged me and those with whom I had had business. I said that, finally, after three months of investigations, Monsieur de La Reynie told me that I had only to stay in my ordinary tranquility, that nothing had been found against me, and that "all would be given back to me," for those were his terms.

The parish priest responded coolly to me that they had plans to put me in Vincennes. "But sir," I said to him, "why not put me rather in the Conciergerie[1] in the hands of Parliament? If I am guilty, I do not ask for grace, but I ask that those who spread calumny would also be punished. It is easy to accuse someone of crimes when one removes from her all means of defending herself, but in a regulated court, like the one in Parliament, the witnesses about whom they were so confident might speak differently, and at least the truth would be known."[2] "You are always in the hands of justice," he responded to me, "because it is Monsieur Desgrez who brought you here, and you are his charge. And since the crimes that you have committed do not merit the death penalty, it is safer to keep you locked up here."

I told him that I would consent to be locked up if they did not form new calumnies to furnish a pretext for it, but that I owed it to God, to piety, to my family and to myself to ask Parliament when everything would be cleared up. He answered me that he would tell Monsieur de Paris this, and that if not for the affair concerning Monsieur de Cambrai,[3] I would already be free. I responded that this affair, which was so strange to me, did not make me more guilty or more innocent, and that if Monsieur de Paris had some proof of crimes against me, as he said, these supposed crimes would not change in nature, depending on the outcome of the affair concerning Monsieur de Cambrai of which he spoke.

He urged me then to avow my crimes to him, saying that God had bestowed an abundance of grace on me, having taken from me the occasion to continue committing them. Then he said that I did not yet have confidence in him, and finally that he found it fair that they should put me in the hands of justice, but that all was well-proven and Monsieur de Paris did not doubt it.

A rather bizarre adventure happened to me at this time. I needed some wine, and, having searched around the place, had found a very good one at one hundred francs per half-barrel. Since I found it a little expensive, I wrote to the man, whose name I will not mention. And I asked him to send it to me if I could not find a better deal, because it was painful to put so much money toward it. Without responding to me, this person sent me a half-barrel at one hundred ecus per barrel, which is to say, at fifty ecus per half-barrel.[4] This seemed extraordinary to me, but I let it go.

A few days later, having wanted to drink some, I found that it burned my mouth, my throat and my bowels with such pains that I thought I would die. I asked someone to go fetch a man from the village who seemed to be a very honest man to see if there was something to be done or if the wine was not yet good to drink. As soon as he tasted it, he appeared frightened and said that only a rogue could have sent this wine, that, as for him, he would not want to drink a half bottle of this, and that he would not taste it without being afraid. He said he was sure that there were added ingredients, and that it would burn the bowels of whoever drank it—all this in front of the girl caring for me who had been desperate to have him come.

They had another owner of a village tavern come who offered to take it at two thirds of the price. He said that he would put it little by little in a mixed wine and would let it be drunk by big cart drivers, mixing it with cassia fruit,[5] and they agreed to this idea. He asked that it be left for a few days in the cellar where it was, but having found it bad after he tasted it, he sent a man who tasted country wines to taste it once again. This man first put some on his hand, and then, having smelled it, did not want to taste it at all and said that it was poisoned wine in front of this girl and several masons who were working. He said that even if he was given as much money as could fit in this cellar, he would not drink it or taste it, and that it was impossible to drink it without dying.

The girl who heard the whole conversation found it truly shocking and went to report it to the parish priest. He told her that if I did not find the wine strong enough, I only had to put less water in it and said that it was necessary that I drink it. She did not dare say anything to him in reply, and, having come to find me, she told me: "Madame, although this might be excellent wine, you must not drink it since it hurts you, but if you want to sell the half-barrel for twenty pounds, they will take it to mix in with a quantity of other wines." I told her that to draw twenty francs from fifty ecus, it was not worth the effort, and that, since it was so excellent, we should simply keep it. It did not bother me to let them have this thorn in their side for having drawn me into such tyranny.

This girl did not dare taste it, saying that she did not have permission. But on the other hand they could not get out of this without having to taste it. It remained this way for a while. Finally, someone came to fetch it at night and switched it with a weak wine that was not worth much. I let them do everything that they wanted, abandoning the future to providence.

Three weeks after having drunk the little bit that I mentioned, my tongue, throat, palate and chest were all still raw. I thought I was going to die one day, and I suffered very great pains in my bowels. Finally, as a result of drinking water, the great fire passed, and I found myself in my ordinary state. This girl seemed afflicted that I had gotten over it.

It sometimes caused me such a great shock to see myself in such hands that I was ready to suffocate from it, but I was no less abandoned to God. I suffered everything without saying anything. Often, I pretended not to see things. They called my patience "crazy." If I showed fear that I might be suspected of something, as I had felt from the beginning, it would be regarded as an extreme fit of anger. So the least word was regarded as a crime; silence and patience were regarded as other crimes.

The parish priest told me something one day that seemed horrible to me for a man of his character, which was that they could not turn me over to the court because they did not have enough of what they needed to have me put to death. Then in changing his opinion, he added: "But it is true that you can always have a proportionate punishment." He had sworn to me by his place in heaven that I would only be there for three months, and that no assumptions would be made about me. My witness and my judge is in heaven. One can fool man, but who can escape the eyes of God?

One thing that caused me a lot of pain was questioning whether, after so many things brought about by the parish priest, I still had to confess myself to him. And I did not think I had to do this. It seemed to me that there was something disgraceful about going to confess to a man who supposed that I committed crimes every day, and from whom I never heard one word of truth.

I nearly lost my sight during that time, and since I could hardly read or work any longer, I lost the only recreation that I could have. I spun sometimes, but very coarsely, this work being still feasible despite my eyes. In order to compensate the girl who had tormented me so much, she was made superior of her order, and another one was put in her place. She had been severely cautioned about me, as far as I could tell at the beginning, but she was a good person who feared God and was a bit scrupulous. She let one of my girls know that if it was thought that she might have the least esteem for me and that I might be happy with her, she would not be left there three days. A little afterwards, she told this girl that she would be obligated through obedience to do things that would displease me and did not want to say what they were. But I learned later that it was to take my girls away from me.

The parish priest, having come on the feast of the Assumption to hear our confession, had Famille[6] go first. The parish priest told her that it was necessary for her to leave, that they wanted to put other girls with me, and that he would get her back to her parents. She responded to him that she had none and was so overcome that she could not tell him another thing. She came back to me more dead than alive to tell me about this.

I then went to confession, and he told me that I would be allowed to have communion the next day. Before leaving, he spoke to me about my mistreatment and told me insultingly: "So your patience is at its end?" wanting to make me understand that I should just prepare myself for more things like those I had already experienced. I answered him, "No, sir, and they will tire of persecuting me rather than my tiring of suffering."

I had great pain from their wanting to take my girls away from me. I feared that this was in order to give me others of whom they were the masters, whom they would make say anything they wanted and who would be rewarded by them. It was a great relief to my mind for me to be able to count on the ones I had, who, being neither traitors nor spies, did not make me pay painful attention to each word I said and did not give sinister interpretations to the most innocent things I might have done.

I still dreamed during this time of things that made an impression of very strong truth on me. It seemed to me that I saw Monsieur Pirot and that he was very cold to me. I told him that I was angry that bad things might have been reported to him about me and that although I might have always noticed that he made efforts to have me stay at Vincennes, I nonetheless did not complain about him. I said that I had explained to N. [La Chétardie] the first time that he was sent to me that my difficulty was that he, Monsieur Pirot, believed that I would not be happy with him. He did not deny having made his plan to have me stay at Vincennes but said that, nevertheless, I was better off in his hands than in those of N. [La Chétardie]. I asked him why Monsieur de Paris was so extremely irritated with me. He answered me that he was only irritated to the extent that N. [La Chétardie] pressed him to be and added: "Go hide, and I will call him."

Then, having had him come, he told him: "So, sir, how do you feel about N. [Madame]?" naming me. The other responded to him, with a gesture and manner that cannot be expressed: "The worst that could be said." And I saw that these gestures and these manners indicated more malice than all that had ever been attributed to him.

I told him, leaving the place where I was: "I will bear witness against you to God's judgment. It is before this formidable judge that I will name you; it is to him that I will ask justice for your malice." As I was talking to him, it seemed as if his priest's habit was changing into large rags of dirty laundry. Someone told me: "Get out, for you are in the worst hands you could ever be in!" A little later, this sister who had been sent to me in place of the first and who was a rather good person came to me, all in tears, to say that she was leaving. She said that she had only done the things that had been asked of her out of obedience, that she had honor and a conscience, that I would see this, and that if she had been willing to betray me for this and that, she would not be leaving. I told her that the worst had been done and I had become used to her, and I asked her to stay. She responded to me that I did not know everything, that the worst must not be allowed to happen, and that she had seen truly terrible things. She said that, as for her, she had no hope of making her fortune and that she did not want to hurt her conscience—all this with the shame of a person who had made some missteps which she had not anticipated, and who was tormented by scruples. Finally, she told me that she was going in order to let the storm pass, and that truly bad things would happen, but that she had no part in them. She begged me to have patience, while swearing to me that she had been made to sign things that she did not understand but that she knew were to my own disadvantage.

I understood from this speech that they had plans to push me to all sorts of extremes, and that, to realize them, they would employ everything that trickery can invent when real proof and reasons are missing. I saw clearly why they were putting all sorts of forces in play and why they were employing so many mechanisms to make me appear guilty and to present me to the public as a person capable of the greatest crimes. But I could not myself imagine that they might be capable of pushing darkness and injustice to the point of authorizing obviously false calumnies, and to do this by inventing acts not only recognized as false, but also invented and suggested by people of questionable character. I swear that I could not have believed that the malice of men could go to such an extreme, if the words that the parish priest would say to me now and again, almost in spite of himself, had not made me judge that there was nothing that one must not fear when a great interest or a strong passion pushes us. However, whatever threats were made to me, I remained at peace, ready for everything and ready for nothing, in the will of my God. If this persecution had concerned me alone I would have suffered less, but since it was only created to envelop people of distinguished merit whom they wanted to oppress by mixing them up with a person so discredited, I would suffer extremely from the displeasure of being the instrument or the pretext for the persecution that they were undergoing. I would sometimes say: "O my God, let everything fall on me, let me be the scapegoat to atone for the faults of your people, but spare the good and do not permit your saints to become food for the birds of the air and the beasts of the earth" (Jer. 7:33). You knew, O my God, which ones were acting according to motives of a bitter zeal and with completely human views, which ones were swept away by a torrent they could not resist that brought them along in spite of themselves, and, finally, which ones became ministers of their passions or weaknesses, in order to please themselves. But you did not know any less those who were made the victims of your truth and have sacrificed everything for it, so as not to betray it at all.

On the eve of All Saints Day, the parish priest, having come to hear my confession, told me that a highly dignified person had furnished testimony by which I was proven guilty of horrible things of which he was a witness. I told him that it was necessary, therefore, that he had come to see me or that I had been to his home, and that this could not be so, given my situation. I said that if they wanted to tell me what had been alleged, it would not be very difficult for me to demonstrate its falsity. He told me again that my faith was in question and that everything that I had signed was completely insincere. I asked him what proof he had of this and who besides himself could be instructed about my feelings, with my only having seen him since I left Vincennes.

He had made these girls believe, at an earlier time, that I was a heretic and that it was due to a true excommunication that communion had been taken away from me. He forbade them to have a priest come to me if some sickness like apoplexy or another one of this nature should befall me, and he said that it was better to let me die without the sacraments because horrible things had recently been discovered about me. When he spoke to me, he made me think that this concerned old crimes. When he spoke to the others, it concerned new ones. This sister about whom I just spoke was only permitted to stay in this house for two months. They did not find her right for their desired purposes, and they made another come from the diocese of Chartres who regarded me as a devil.

The parish priest brought me a *Pastoral Instruction* from Monsieur de Paris, which he made me understand I must accept. Since the work was long, I asked him to give me some time to read it. His intention in asking for this consent from me was not difficult to see. The *Pastoral Instruction* was so full of artifices and interpretations so contrary to the feelings that I had had all of my life, that I would have accepted the most horrible death rather than an imputation so contrary to the purity of my faith. I made him understand in a very firm way that I would never accept such a thing, and that he should desist from this. He told me that I should at least write a letter to Monsieur de Paris, who had ordered him to make me read this pastoral letter in which I was so implicated. I told him that I would do this willingly, and I sent it to him a few days later in these terms:

> Monsignor, I have read with all possible respect and submission the pastoral letter that Your Greatness has given me through the parish priest. There are two things, Monsignor. The first concerns what my ignorance, my confusions, my lack of illumination and the lack of knowledge I have of the meanings of terms and their implications made me put in my books, not penetrating the improper interpretations that one can give them. This, Monsignor, is what I submit, such as I have said and concerning which I have already given all the testimony possible, as truly catholic, not only to the Church and to the Sovereign Pontiff, but also to you, Monsignor, with all the sincerity and humiliation of which a completely Christian heart is capable, not wanting to have any particular sentiments, and not having any others, except those of the Church.

The other article, Monsignor, concerns the sentiment that Your Greatness imputes to me. I want to believe that my ignorance and my poor ways of expressing myself gave Your Greatness a reason to draw conclusions so far from the sentiments that I have always had, through the grace of God. I must, however, point out to Your Greatness, with very profound respect and protesting even in the presence of Our Lord Jesus Christ, who knows that I am not lying at all, that I have never had such sentiments, that I do not have them at all and that I never will have them, if it pleases God, that I even have an extreme horror of them, such as I have always protested to Your Greatness and to all those who have asked me for the reasoning behind my faith, having always been ready to shed my blood for all the truths taught by the catholic and apostolic Roman Church.

I am truly miserable after having so many times declared my sentiments, which no one can know but myself, concerning the articles that have been imputed to me, which, nevertheless, I have always sworn not to have at all. And I am all the more unhappy for having to say, in spite of my good will, the righteousness of my intentions, and my sincere desire to be with God and to do all things for his glory, that writing has been attributed to me about sentiments so contrary to those that I have always had.

As for what concerns my contemplative prayer, I have tried to perform it as best I could to make God happy, but since it is not for me to judge what is best and most useful, I have offered several times to the parish priest, who hears my confession by your order, to do it as he would judge appropriate. I renew this offer to you, Monsignor, assuring Your Greatness that I am and will always be ready to do this as it will be ordered, according to my power, submitting all my soul and my weak lights and the most tender sentiments of my heart, to obedience. I would prefer never to perform contemplative prayer rather than to oppose what I am ordered to do. I believe that contemplative prayer from one's own will would hardly please God, and since I desire nothing other than to please him and to do his holy will, I am indifferent about the choice of the means. I will always submit them to the great heart of Y[our] G[reatness]. I do this, Monsignor, both through duty and through inclination, having as much respect as submission, etc. December, 1697.

The parish priest, after having read my letter, summoned me to say that it was good. It is not easy to reconcile this idea with the treatment that I received from him. Sometimes he declared that he was working to have me go to my son's house, and then he assured the sisters, conversely, that I would die with them. One of them told me this in confidence. So much bad treatment and continual harassment saddened me to excess at certain moments, but I showed nothing. And I even reproached myself for this sadness, as unworthy of the sacrifice that I had so often made to God with my whole self and out of the love that he had given me for the cross.

I went for a rather long time without seeing the parish priest, which I did not know how to explain. Finally, he came and affected much honesty toward me. He told me that Monsieur de Paris was very happy with my letter and assured me of his consideration. Experience had taught me more than once that it was when he was very gentle that I had the most to fear and he was plotting the most. He ordered that I be allowed to receive communion on Sundays and all feast days, after having left me for three months without permitting them to me. These highs and lows were very suspicious to me, and I waited in peace for what providence would order.

I was made to see a book during this time that tore me apart in a strange way. It was composed by a monk of merit, the friend of a prelate who had regarded me highly, and who had changed his feelings since then for reasons that I have explained earlier.[7] This good monk, cautioned by the stories of all kinds that had been made up about me, and even more by his conversations with this prelate, his friend, which he reports, believing himself to serve God and the Church, gave to the public ideas about me that he had formed. I hope that God will hold him accountable for his good intentions.

But without going into a rebuttal of the things that he was reporting, the truth is that Father La Combe did not stay with me at all in Grenoble. He came there twice in twenty-four hours on behalf of Monsignor, the Bishop of Verceil, to propose that I go see him. I was in Lyon for a short time, about twelve days, with Madame Belof, a woman of merit known in the entire city for her virtue and her piety, who stayed at the home of Monsieur Thomé, her father, where I saw almost no one. And I never got dressed to be out in public. One can impose such opinions on people who never have known me at any time and who have never seen me.

All the rest of the story of this good monk was no truer, since I have never been made to leave any diocese, and Monsieur de Grenoble himself asked me to establish myself in Grenoble. I have never seen in Lyon a servant who was fifty years old or of any other age, and I do not know any. Monsieur de Geneva told me himself what Father La Combe had told him on God's behalf (for this is how he expressed himself) two or three years before I was in his diocese.

And in recounting it to me, he told me: "I felt that he was telling me the truth, and that he was telling me things that only God and I knew." This did not prevent him from giving him to me as Director when he engaged me to work at establishing the New Catholics of Gex. I have spoken earlier about all that.[8]

When I was put in Saint Mary, Monsieur the Official was told that I was always disheveled, and that even the hollows in my stomach could be seen. When he saw me dressed as I always am and as I always have been since my youth, he remained so surprised that he could not prevent himself from commenting on it, and he spoke about it to Mother Eugenie[9] too.

I have also made note of what made me leave Verceil and the friendship that this prelate had for me. The nun with whom this good monk said, further, that I had business, and who passes for holy in the order of Saint Ursula, and who is called the Good Mother, had died a year before I was in this country. She put down some writings about truth, but they are all enlightened.

I do not understand how this good—moreover, so respectable—monk was able to resolve himself to turn out all sorts of inanities concerning vague and uncertain reports, unless he only believed himself to give glory to God by defaming a person who was considered so dangerous and so capable of doing harm. I ask only that attention be paid to the people who have been considered my friends all my life, whom I have seen and treated with familiarity. It will be easy to judge the reason that so many lies and so many calumnies have been issued.

I am omitting a lot of very big things in order to abridge, only writing this much due to my weakness, and only taking it up a little at a time, so that sometimes I only write a half page each day, and I only write from pure truth, with a lot of repugnance. And far from exaggerating, I diminish a lot. I believe that without the trial that was conducted in Rome, I would not have been tormented as much. As it was told to me later, after all of his affairs were finished, I was rendered more despicable, and I was accused of more opprobrium and of all sorts of infamy, and this was believed more or, to speak more correctly, they flattered themselves more by dazzling the public with the haughty and violent procedures with which they pressed for this affair, which had been brought to Rome from the beginning. And they pretended to make part of the indignation that had been felt toward me fall on Monsieur de Cambrai because he had appeared to esteem me and he was believed to be one of my friends.

A coarse peasant who worked as a servant to this sister who guarded me, not having any interest in persecuting me, was horrified to see everything that they did to me and could not stop herself from saying this to her confessor, who developed considerable esteem for me from this. And I have since received all of the services that he could offer. Since a lot of poor people often came to the house, I had them given some alms by this sister who, in the expenses she would write down, put down the sum for charity. Monsieur de Saint Sulpice, having learned of this, forbade her from putting it in the ledger as an expense, and said that it was forbidden for it to appear as if I were doing any good at all. This was moved under other expenses, and I agreed that the alms that I was giving were passed on as being from the sisters, but a lot of people did not believe me. There were a lot of wounded people who came to have their wounds treated at this home. The sisters did not want to do this at all. They asked me to do it, and I healed them.

4

The Confessor

AFTER HAVING REMAINED for about twenty months in this house, where I suffered all that can be imagined, I received a very important letter from the parish priest. I found a way to send this letter to a person whom I trusted to keep it for me. For although it was written with much malice and bitterness, one will be perhaps surprised that all the crimes, old and new, about which they spoke to me all the time and the proof of which, they said, was so clear and so certain, with which they entertained the public with such artfulness and such care, that these crimes, I say, only ended up being read in newspapers of all kinds, from the fairy tales that were classified as novels, to eating green peas, to drinking wine from Alicante, to having a little dog and a little parakeet, and other things of this nature that one will see in this letter, which I want to put down here in order to diminish none of the things of which they wanted to accuse me.

What one will find difficult to imagine but will have even more difficulty understanding, is that in this same letter he assures me that he will treat me justly, believing me very far away from the unfortunate maxims that are attributed to the Quietists, which were the basis for so many of the persecutions that it was necessary for me to suffer for fifteen or sixteen years and for which they saw fit to defame me like the worst of creatures.

Here is the letter:

Madame,
Here is a letter that is going to surprise you, but I can no longer hide from you the pain that your behavior causes me. The true reasons that I believe myself to have for it have multiplied so much and appear so considerable to me that there are no means to tolerate them anymore without explaining myself to you. The zeal that I must have for your salvation, the obligation that I have to live up to the confidence that Monsignor the Arch[bishop] showed me in confiding you to my care, the interests of the Church, and several other

important reasons move me to open up my heart to you, since you have not opened yours up to me. And to tell you the truth, I would believe myself to have betrayed you if I stayed silent any longer. He who sees the most secret intentions is my witness that I only come here to satisfy my conscience, which presses me on, and so as not to attract any reproach from this just Judge, who requires one to submit an exact report of the lights and the movements that he gives for the direction of the souls with which one is charged. I have even withdrawn from you more than ordinarily in these last few months, not being able to resolve to administer the sacraments to you in the state of blindness and false peace in which you appear to me to be. Here is, then, Madame, what gives me much trouble concerning you, and what should not cause you any less. And I beg you to undertake tranquil and serious reflection before God upon this, as upon the thing in the world that is most important to you, which it is of the utmost importance for us not to misunderstand. I protest to you again once more that only charity and the pure desire to be useful to you open my mouth, and they only open it for me as I am after many prayers and requests reiterated to God not to permit me to trouble you wrongly on this question or to tell you anything except in his Spirit. I flatter myself that I will perhaps be satisfying God because I testify for myself that no person in the world and no human view made me act on this occasion.

First, Madame, how can true and solid piety be in accord with the spirit of presumption and self-esteem? You have told me, among other things, and this in conversation and in precise words, that from your youth, although you might have been beautiful, you have always lived in innocence; that you had won souls over to God, especially young women of quality at the Court, which attracted the indignation of many people toward you; that you were a servant of God; that you were dear to God; and that God was being mistreated through your person.

You have even written this to me, I think. And if I had not recaptured these dangerous instances of self-satisfaction by order of Monsignor the Arch[bishop] himself, who had enjoined me to do so, I believe that you might have continued to add others—that, besides, one had treated you more harshly by making you suffer what you endured than by cutting off your head, because at least you would be dead as a martyr. And if I am not mistaken, you might have added: "in truth."

More than once in my presence, at Vincennes, you allowed your chambermaid to say haughtily and arrogantly that in you I was seeing the holiest person on earth, and that it was not necessary for Monsignor the Arch[bishop] to have compassion for your suffering, but for one to have compassion for him, since he persecuted a saint as great as you without reason. It is true that, while laughing, you told her to withdraw.

What will I say of the acts of anger and indignation, not to mention the temper tantrums, which have been so strong and so frequent in you, since I have had the honor to know you, that it is truly hard to believe. And I can say that I have hardly seen wilder fits in people who are the quickest to anger and the most passionate in the world! How many times did I need to keep silent, to conceal and to suppress things in order not to irritate you! You have told me, during one of these moments, that you would like to present a petition to the King so that you might be tried, and so that it might be decided whether you were guilty or not. But you said that you did not want to be judged by priests or people of the Church, because they did not have the probity or good faith found in laics, and you objected also to the commissioners and said that only Parliament was sufficient for you. Once you wrote me two letters while visibly transported by passion. You showed them, as I learned later, to the good sisters staying with you, and these sisters suggested that you suppress them, but futilely. It was necessary to follow your mood in preference to this good advice. You put in one of these letters, among other things, that if I did not do the things you asked of me, you would pray to God requesting that he make me feel what you were to Him, saying that I mistreated God in you, and asking that he not pardon me. Who ever made such prayers to God? And since when does a penitent woman tell her confessor in this manner which way is useful to her? When someone wanted to block a window and a door in the back of your apartment, which you yourself should have wanted, what fire, what indignation did you not show? You opposed this with such force, you and your chambermaids, that it was necessary then to leave them as they were and give in until your emotion ceased. They waited until you became calm again and capable of understanding reason. On the occasion that the good sisters who kept you guarded did not want to permit you to be seen through the window of their apartment, which looks out over the street where there were a lot of people, you and your girls, how did you treat them? Let us forget the hurtful words that you said to them, although they assured you that they were only operating this way because your superiors ordered it thus. But what is yet more shocking is that you might have added that you were in a convent where, although the bishop of the place had forbidden the sisters to allow you to have certain things, they did not stop letting you have them in spite of his prohibition. In truth, Madame, are these the speech and thoughts of a soul who, setting herself up as a mistress of the spiritual life, undertakes to teach others a *Short and Easy Method to Arrive in a Short Time to the Highest Perfection*?

After this, how blind would you be, Madame, if you did not become suspect to yourself, and if you still thought yourself to be a prophet? You know it, Madame, and the thing is too important and too apt to have thought to omit here, whatever pain it might cause you. In the month of August in the year 1696, during two visits that I made to you within eight days, you told me positively—and this at Vincennes, where you had no human way to learn what was going on in the world—you assured me, I say, that you had had two types of visions or revelations—call them what you will. In these you came to know that we were on the eve of seeing great revolutions, that the King was supposed to die soon, that it was necessary to alert Madame de Maintenon, Monsieur de Beauvillier, and Monsieur the Bishop of Cambrai with diligence, that there was not one moment to lose, and that it was a question of the salvation of the King's soul. You wanted to write to Monsieur de Cambrai. You charged me to deliver the letter to him as soon as possible. You wanted me to declare this important secret out loud to an important person. You assured me that when you had these sorts of revelations one by one and at two different times, it was a sign of certainty. However, Madame, all this was an illusion. The month of September passed. The King, thank heaven, remained healthy, and it was necessary to blush with shame.

And when afterwards I wanted to use this splendid prediction, so certain, so pressing, so well-written, to bring you to suspect your lights and your own mind, how confused and bewildered you seemed! You might nevertheless have imagined yourself capable of finding some way of responding to an uncertain future, and thus you told me that the month of September 1697 had not yet come. What a pity! But things remain now as they have been for a long time, and there is nothing to say to you except this word of warning from Scripture to the false prophets. For this is not even the only false prophecy that you have made that was not fulfilled, as your best friends admit. *One can be assured that it is not the Lord who has spoken through him, and that the depravity of his arrogant heart seduces him; this is why you will not fear vain predictions at all.*[1]

But Madame, what is there to say about the story of your *Life* that you have written, full of such fanciful visions that you yourself would not be able to tolerate reading it, nor would your greatest friends without confusion, nor would anyone without indignation? You have even dared to compose several *Commentaries on the Scripture*, most certainly full of errors. You are always ready to condemn them with the same ease that you have had in composing them, or at least you affirm this to be the case. Have you not ceaselessly maintained that one can find nothing bad in your works except some terms or expressions in which your judgment was able to hide the meaning and the force? But, as for the rest, you have maintained that you have found your doctrine in the books of the greatest saints of the Church, that you are ready to justify yourself, that you did not have a single retraction to make except in the words, and that one must not speak to you about other things? These are your own terms, written the same day as you uttered them with a lot of emotion.

I swear that after this you signed a rather formal disavowal of your errors, but in good faith, Madame, are you convinced deep down that you have written them? Do you detest them truly? Do you regret having spread dangerous maxims, having harmed many people who believed you too easily, and being the cause of a great part of the distressing division that presently troubles the Church? Not at all, you give no sign of it. And you have testified many times in great tranquility that you have no doubts about anything, and that you are such as you were before. All that happened is reckoned by you as null and void. You are always a persecuted saint, as your two chambermaids proclaim, and there is nothing to rebuke in your behavior or to reform in your books but terms whose significance was unknown to you. But, Madame, who would believe that a person like yourself, who speaks your natural tongue so well and who professes to be so well instructed in mystical theology, might be ignorant of what French words of devotion mean? Is it to excuse your errors that you cover them with a veil of beautiful, and very coarse, ignorance? If you are really as ignorant as that, as you affirm, why do you get mixed up in preaching dogma, teaching, and publicizing your new doctrines in the Church, which you see causing such scandals here? Let yourself be silent, in accord with the established order of the Apostle,[2] so as to learn the orthodox doctrine, especially as a teacher, as you have done only too much.

Further, Madame, from where did you draw this sublime theology that the most enlightened saints have taught us, and in what works do you boastfully claim to find your doctrine? Who would not be surprised to learn that in nearly two years you have not asked for a single book of devotion? Who would believe that a soul, which claims to be raised to a high level of perfection, united to God through a love so pure, and favored with the gift of contemplation and prophetic visions, might have read for over a year the news of the world at large, the newspapers of France, of Flanders, and of Holland, the journals of the Savants,³ the *Mercure Galant*, Aesop's Fables in verse, and novels full of amorous intrigue, of which the title alone would put off not only people who are pious, but people who are moderately well-behaved and modest? How did you not have any scruples, Madame, about keeping books and novellas for such a long time, sending for them regularly, filling your imagination with them, and reading them so avidly that the Lenten season and even the eve of Palm Sunday could not make you put the brakes on it? Your excesses have been tolerated because one wanted to see to what point your dissipation would go, in order then to obligate you to return to yourself and make you feel that you are other than you believe.

What would be said, Madame, if your life was known to be so little filled with mortification and so subject to the satisfaction of the senses that there should not be the appearance of permitting the frequent use of the sacraments by whomever would live like this? How much have we been pained to find you having the best wine in all of Paris! The one that cost twenty *sous* per pint was not excellent enough; your stomach suffered, you said. It was necessary to buy some at forty or fifty *sous* per half-barrel, often gotten from the wine shop and in notable quantities. Who would not be a little astonished to learn that you drank fashionable liqueurs, wine from Alicante, and even wine from Spain, or that you took tobacco in significant quantities, and that the last box you were sent cost nine francs? Who would think that a person so dead to earthly tastes took care to go out looking for the best fowl, to eat the best meat from the butcher shop and the best fish, to have the first new fruits, asparagus, green peas, artichokes, to spend entire days in the garden during the summer, to make the pot boil and to cook her dinner there—although this engendered the fear that you would cause a fire in the little woods of the house where you lived—to amuse yourself with linnets⁴ and turtledoves, with dogs and parakeets, and other seeming silliness, to have conceived of the idea, in the state you were in, to put—or to have someone put—money into the lottery in Paris, where you disguised your name under the alias "The Unfortunate Woman," to have won some paintings there so dishonestly that it was necessary to trade them for other things, as you have told me you wanted to settle this. I am only going into such specific detail, Madame, out of compulsion and in spite of myself, and nothing obligates me to do so except the desire to make you understand that you are not as you think and as you have led others to think about you.

And yet these trifles here are not criminal, and some of these diversions can be permitted, especially to a woman of your condition, of your good fortune, and of your age. And your health requires a few of them. However, Madame, when one allows oneself these things, one must not put oneself on par with an extraordinary person or flatter oneself to have a sublime perfection. One must descend from the pretentious elevation, putting oneself on the level of the simple faithful, who walk on the common path and who limit themselves to the observation of precepts, and no longer setting oneself up as a mistress of the spiritual life, which is found in *A Short and Easy Method,* to show the most eminent holiness. And this is where you claimed to be, Madame. For inclining to suspect that you might be in the nascent error of those who maintain that by giving one's spirit to God one time, one can then wound true piety and satisfy one's sensuality, God forbid, Madame, that I have thought this of you.

But I well know that, even in the midst of their infirmities and the harshest persecution, those whom one honors as saints still led penitent and mortified lives, that they would perform contemplative prayer ceaselessly, that they provided rare examples of patience and humility. These saints would have believed themselves lost if, especially in those times of trials and tribulation, they had let themselves fall into a laxity that would not be tolerated, in whomever it might be, even in a community with little regulation, and who without a doubt surprised and poorly edified both those on the outside and those on the inside, the house into which you had withdrawn not being able to accord you such a life with the high perfection which you claimed to profess. For you are quite right, Madame, that all this could not remain a secret and that it was necessary that various people who serve your needs knew about it, and that these things passed through their hands and before their eyes. And do not complain, Madame, that I tell you perhaps too much. Be fair and be a witness to yourself that I suppress many important accusations from which I want to spare you.

Indeed, it is right that I stop here because I know the extreme pain that reading this letter will cause you, but I also know the indispensable obligation that I have to write it to you. The doctor who spares healthful remedies to his patient because they are bitter or painful is cruel, and the one who gives them is charitable. You know, Madame, how many times I have told you that providence permitted you to come to your present solitude in order to reflect more seriously on your conscience and to remedy it effectively. I have told you that your salvation was attached to the good use made of this very sweet and comfortable retreat that had been happily procured for you; that you have been offered all sorts of help for that purpose; that you should make a very exact account to God of it, as the happiest time of your life; and that I clear my conscience by telling this to you and that I could do no more.

Were all the means, all the advances very successful? You know it, Madame. But in truth I believe myself totally useless to your well-being if you do not want to make greater use of them, and if you are set on staying where you are. I beg you, Madame, to recognize yourself, to humiliate yourself, to confess the truth, to enter into the true feelings of penitence, to avow your errors in good faith, to lament the scandal and the division that you have, in large part, caused in the Church. Without this, Madame, I would be a blind guide, and I would respond to God with the lethargic languor into which I believe you have plunged. I would ask permission from Monsignor the Arch[bishop] to find it proper that I withdraw and to give you a man more enlightened than I, who might have more influence on your spirit, and for whom you might have more consideration, so that you might suspect him less of acting for political reasons and in pursuit of human esteem.

For, Madame, to whom do you mean to address these words that you wrote, more than a year ago, in large letters on the door of the little grotto in your garden, if it is not me? Here they are: "The coward follows fortune and the unhappy one is worthy of respect" (Seneca). After that, how could a director be useful to you? How would you have faith in him? Moreover, how to refrain from believing that you always see yourself as a persecuted, innocent person and think that you suffer for justice and consequently are repentant of nothing, when one reads once more the other words that you have written in capital letters in relation to the preceding ones, by which you meant without a doubt to refer to yourself: "As they have persecuted me they will persecute you, and they will believe themselves to serve God by persecuting you" (Jesus Christ) (John 15:20).

Such is the idea that you have of yourself and the spirit of great sorrow by which you are animated. It is therefore appropriate, Madame, that, being no longer good for anything to you, I withdraw at the pleasure of

Monsignor the Arch[bishop], without ceasing nevertheless to feel a true charity in accord with God, Madame, your very humble and very obedient servant. J. de La Ch[étardie], parish priest of St. S[ulpice]."

The reproaches of which this letter is full and the wicked twists that are used there taught me nothing new about the negative disposition that the parish priest had toward me, and the one that he had inspired in Monsieur de Paris. For a long time I had known what to prepare myself for. My continuous illnesses and the anguish of such a long captivity—felt by the poor girls who served me with such affection when they found themselves at their wits' end—were able to authorize a lot of things or to excuse them, if the things for which this letter reproached me were explored in some detail. But I leave all this aside, as a stranger to the motives behind my many years of imprisonment and the more than eighty interrogations, of eight to ten hours for the most part, that it was necessary to suffer.

I will say only in passing that the parish priest himself had pressed me several times to read the newspapers and that he had gotten angry when I had not wanted to do it. The novels were fairy tales that he himself brought me from my daughter, and my women sometimes had fun reading them for hours on end as a diversion. Moreover, I read the history of the Church of Joseph, and I had more than fifty books of devotion, which we read nearly continuously: the Bible, the New Testament, the Lives of the Saints, etc. We fasted every Friday and Saturday of the year, all of Lent, and twelve days in Advent. But when a heart is indisposed concerning a certain point, the same things that could edify become a cause for scandal, and the eye receptive to only one color sees this same color in all objects.

This letter was brought to me by this sister who guarded me. She had been ordered to observe me reading it to see if I was strongly afflicted or if I got angry. I did not say one word to this girl, and I interacted with her with the usual gaiety. She began to cry, and I consoled her, assuring her that I did not attribute to her the malevolence of that with which she had been charged.

She told me that she had undergone a terrible interrogation with the parish priest about me, and that he had asked her if I had ever spoken to her of God, to which she had responded no. "Swear then that she is ungodly," he told her. "Sir," she answered him, "since I have cold feet, and she had a nice fire, I was there sometimes to warm up. The Lives of the Saints would be read in her room, and we sometimes spoke of some of the circumstances of those lives." "But then she spoke about God," he said. "Yes sir," answered this girl. "That is all I wanted to know. She preached dogma, and that is all that

I wanted." Whatever this sister might have said, though only being in the form of a conversation, it was necessary to sign it.

The peasant who answered coarsely that she knew nothing but good was also interrogated. He told her that she was only an animal. And she told him that she did not have enough intelligence to see evil. He chased her away with insults. She spoke about this to her confessor, who ordered her to tell it to me.

The same methods had been used with the first sister who had tormented me so much and who was so strongly devoted to them. They made her sign a lot of things without telling her what they were, half with threats, half with promises. She would only do it if they took her to see Monsieur de Paris, who made her the Superior General of her Congregation. I believe that I have already said this because I do not report things in the order in which they happened but in the way they come to mind. This girl was not, however, so lacking in conscience that she did not have some terrible remorse. Crying, she came to find me one day and told me that they had made her sign a lot of things against me without her reading them. She said that if something bad should happen to me, and they produced her signature, I should ask to confront her, and she would say that they had forced her to sign them.

But they never did talk to me about these things, any more than all the others, in the interrogations that they made me undergo afterwards. They only wanted to deceive the public without letting me know for fear that I might try to justify myself. Maybe they wanted to procure for future use a justification of such violent and despicable behavior, for which they might be reproached one day, God knows.

The peasant told me one day that, having gone to the home of the parish priest on behalf of this sister, he had made her stay in his room, believing her so stupid that he actually thought that she would be unable to understand anything that was happening. It was a writing specialist, the same forger who was discussed so much later in my life. And this girl noticed very clearly that someone's writing was being forged. The parish priest told him: "this letter is not formed well; he does not form his L's like you." She again spoke about this to her confessor, who ordered her to tell it to me.

5

The False Letter

A FEW DAYS after this important letter, Monsieur de Paris came to see me with pomp and circumstance. He entered my room with the parish priest, who was in despair that I should appear so disinterested. He sat down and made the parish priest sit down next to him. And since I put myself in a place with my back to the light, he made me face the light because he wanted to see my face.

He forced himself to speak to me sweetly at first and told me: "I have come to put you back on good terms with the parish priest who complains so much about you, and who no longer wants to be your confessor." I responded to him: "Monsignor, I do not believe myself to have given him any reason to complain about me, and I will confess myself to him through obedience."

That was all. For I am persuaded, without flattering myself, that someone other than me would not have confessed to him after having learned that this man was only working for my downfall. But since he had been dressed up in sacred robes, I believed myself to confess to my dear Master by confessing to him. And I had always felt that he would speak to me so differently in the confessional than he did elsewhere, and this confirmed for me the promise of Jesus Christ, who often permitted a bad priest to bless him, for he would confess himself to a bad one and let him say what he pleased. I do not judge this one here at all. I am only relating historical facts that I swear on the Bible.

To get back to what I was saying, Monsieur de Paris told me: "but if he does not give you confession, no one will want to give you confession!" "Monsignor," I told him, "the Jesuits would give me confession if I was free." This put him in a very bad mood.

He wanted to have me make a public declaration that I had committed all kinds of shameful debaucheries with Father La Combe and made terrible threats against me if I did not declare that I had imposed on good people, that I had tricked them and that I was engaged in debauchery when I had done my writing. Finally, he demonstrated anger that I never would have expected from a man who had previously seemed to me to be so measured. He assured me that he would destroy me if I did not do what he wanted.

I told him that I knew all about his high social standing. For it is necessary to note that the parish priest had taken great care to notify me of his favor. He had informed me that his nephew had been married to the niece of Madame de Maintenon, that the King had given him the shirt,[1] which he only did to Princes, that he had given him a lot in recognition of this marriage, in a word, all that could give me a good idea of the consideration that the King gave to him in public. But God knows the attention that I give to earthly fortunes. I responded to him that he could destroy me if he wanted to and that this would only happen to me if it pleased God. He told me on this point above, "I would prefer to hear you say, I am at the point of desperation, rather than to hear you speak of the will of God." "But, Madame," the parish priest said to me, "swear, Madame, that when you wrote your books, you were engaged in debauchery!" "I would be lying to the Holy Spirit," I answered him, "if I swore such a lie." "We know what La Maillard said," added Monsieur de Paris. (This is this glove maker who was already mentioned from the time I was put with the Daughters of St. Marie). She said, "Sir, could you rely on an unfortunate woman who jumped over the walls of her cloister, where she was a nun, in order to lead an excessive life, of which there is proof such as her running off, and who finally got married, and the rest of her frightening story?" He said to me, "She will go straight to paradise and you to hell. We have the power to bind and loose." "But sir," I answered him, "what do you want me to do? I am only trying to please you, and I am ready for everything, provided that I do not wound my conscience." He answered me that he wanted me to swear that I had been engaged in debauchery my whole life, and that if I did that, he would protect me and would tell the whole world that I had converted. I made him see the impossibility of my swearing to such a lie, and after that he took out a letter that he told me was from Father La Combe.

He read it to me and then told me: "You see that the father swears to have had liberties with you that could rise to the level of sin." I felt no confusion or surprise from this letter. Having gotten close enough for me to look it over, I noticed that he was carefully hiding the address, and even the writing appeared forged to me, although with a certain resemblance. I answered that if the Father had written this letter, he must have gone crazy, or the power of torture had made him write it. He told me, "The letter is from him." "If it is from him," I said, "Sir, he only has to confront me. This is the way to find the truth."

The parish priest began speaking and had me understand that they would not take that path because Father La Combe only canonized me and that they would not want to have this affair judged, but that he would bring witnesses who would show proof of my guilt.

Monsieur de Paris backed up his speech. I told him that that being the case, I would not tell him one word. He added that they would truly make me talk. "No," I told him, "I can be made to endure whatever one wants, but nothing is capable of making me talk when I do not want to."

He told me that it was he who had made me leave Vincennes. I responded to him that I had cried in leaving it because I knew well that I would only be removed from this place to be put in another where I could be accused of crimes. He told me that he knew well that I had cried while leaving there, that it was my friends who had asked him to take charge of me, and that without this I would have been sent much further. To this I answered that it would have been a great pleasure.

So he told me that he was fed up with me. I told him, "Sir, you could be delivered from me if you wanted, and if it were not for the deep respect that I have for you, I would tell you that I have my own pastor to whom you might entrust me." He appeared embarrassed, and he told me that he did not know what to do, and that with the parish priest no longer wanting to give me confession, he could find no one who wanted to be charged with me. And approaching me, he said in a low voice, "You will be destroyed." I told him in a loud voice, "You have all the power, sir; I am in your hands. You have all your social standing; I have only my life to lose." "One does not want to take away your life," he told me; "you would believe yourself a martyr, and your friends would believe it too; it is necessary to set the record straight."

Then, he made me swear by the living God, as if on Judgment Day, to say whether I ever had the least and slightest liberty with Father La Combe. I told him with my frankness and my ingenuousness, which cannot lie, that when he arrived after a trip, after not having seen him for a long time, he gave me a kiss, holding my head in his hands; this was done with an extreme simplicity, and was so for me as well. He asked me if I had gone to confession about this. I told him no and that, not believing anything wrong, the thought had not even come to mind, since he was not just greeting me but everyone else present whom he knew. "Swear then," said the parish priest, "that you have lived in debauchery." "I could never tell such a lie, sir," I responded to him, "and what I told you has nothing to do with debauchery and is far from it." If these are not the exact words, they are at least the gist of it.

Since I was talking with much respect to Monsieur de Paris, he told me, "Ah! My God, Madame, not so much respect, and more humility and obedience!" There was another time when, alluding to the excess of his pain, he told me, "I am your arch[bishop]. I have the power to damn you; yes, I damn you!" I replied to him, smiling, "Sir, I hope that God will have more indulgence and that he will not confirm this sentence." He told me further that my daughters were enduring martyrdom for me, and that, therefore, I was seducing those who had known me. At another time, while asking me to sign a statement that I had committed crimes and enormous sins, he invoked the humility of St. Francis, who would say the same thing of himself. When I said that I had not done this at all, I was accused of pride and of callousness, and told that if I had sworn in the manner of St. Francis, I would have been commended to the public for acknowledging having committed these crimes.

He asked me again whether I was sure that grace was in me. I responded to this question that no one knows if he is worthy of love or of hate. He reproached me for the story of my *Life* and wanted to make me write that the desire to garner praise for myself had led me to write all the lies of which the book is full.

He reproached me for having taken the best meat and examined the sister's book about what had been bought for my food: fowl, wine—nothing was forgotten. In truth everything was taken in excess, and I remember a great list on which there were chickens, pigeons and capons, thirty-six soles. The wine containing quinine that they had gotten, which I took almost constantly because of a continually recurring fever, was exaggerated as if I drank it in excess. But I did not open my mouth in reply to all that.

Finally after many threats and angry episodes that I was made to experience, Monsieur de Paris left, and the parish priest, remaining behind, told me: "Here is the copy of Father La Combe's letter. Read it carefully, write me directly and I will help you." I did not give him any reply, and Monsieur de Paris sent for it to get it back. Here is a copy of that letter:

It is before God, Madame, that I sincerely acknowledge that there has been illusion, error and sin in certain things that happened with too much liberty between us, and I reject and detest all principles and behavior that depart from the commandments of God and of the Church, strongly disavowing all that I might have done or said against these sacred and inviolable laws, and exhorting you in Our Lord to do the same. I do this so that you and I might repair as much as possible the harm that could have been caused by our bad example or by all that we have written that could cause the least damage to the moral rules professed by the Holy Catholic Church, to whose authority, under the judgment of the prelates, we must submit all spiritual doctrine, of whatever degree one claims it to be. Once more, I beg you, by the love of Jesus Christ, that we might have recourse to the only remedy of penitence, and that, by a life truly repentant and upstanding at every point, we might erase the unfortunate impressions caused in the Church by our false steps. Let us humbly confess, you and me, our sins before heaven and earth; let us not blush to have committed them and not avowed them. What I declare to you here comes from my complete frankness and freedom. And I ask God to inspire in you the same sentiments that he seems to me to have welcomed by his grace, which I hold myself obligated to uphold.

Done on April 27, 1698. Signed Dom François de La Combe, Barnabite.

I asked to see this letter, which had been read to me by Monsieur de Paris. He showed it to me with much difficulty. Finally, with him always holding it and not wanting to put it in my hands, for an instant I saw the writing, which seemed to me rather forged. I believed that it was of great importance to seem not to recognize that the letter from Father La Combe was forged until they confronted me with it when I was in prison, and I believed that it would be more advantageous for me to have the lie known at that time. This impelled me to say simply that if the letter was from him, he must have gone crazy over the sixteen years since I had last seen him, or that unbearable judicial torture might have made him say such a thing.

But after they left, and I read the copy that the parish priest had left me, I did not at all doubt that the letter was forged, and that this copy itself was the original because someone had corrected a "v" that was not made in the same way as the Father's.

To say all that went through my mind at the end of this conversation is not possible for me. It is certain that the respect that I believed myself to owe a man of this character prevented me from denying it to his face or making him understand that I saw the falseness to its full extent and the indignity of the trap that he was setting for me. But I could not resolve myself to show him such scorn. Furthermore, letting him assume that I believed the letter legitimate might make him more audacious in making it public, which would give me the occasion to make its falseness known to the world and to have the text judged by a sample.

For what would be more natural for justifying so much violence and for not letting the people who held me in high regard continue to have any room to do so than to try me on the basis of such documents and with witnesses so capable of setting the record straight? The public, so prejudiced, would have seized upon the least appearance of guilt from this, and in order to make my friends—who were possessed so strongly in their hearts, they said—join in their prejudice, these friends would have had no reply and would have had to be the first ones to throw stones at me for having tricked them under a false veil of piety. All would be finished. And one would never have been able to give enough praise to those who would have rendered such a service to the Church: here is what righteousness would have inspired in them.

But what will perhaps appear incredible is that, after having spread this supposed letter from Father La Combe all over Paris and from there to the provinces, as a proof of the errors of Quietism and at the same time as a justification of the supervision that was undertaken in my case in sending me to the Bastille, neither this letter nor my relationship with Father La Combe was ever in question in all of the interrogations that I had to endure. This again is truly certain proof that they were only looking to shape opinion in the public, and even more in Rome, by mixing up the affairs of Monsieur de Cambrai with my own, in order to make him detestable to this Court. And they were looking to justify the fuss that was made through views that have nothing to do with me. I keep silent.

Still another proof that Father La Combe could not have written this letter is that in this conversation I was made to understand that he would canonize me. What relation is there between such excessive praise and a letter that suggests crimes! It is not even in his style, and it is easy to see in it an affectation in the terms appropriate to the effect for which it was composed.

Moreover, Father La Combe, who heard my confession for such a long time and who knew about the innermost recesses of my heart, could not have written such a letter without being the vilest of all men. But I am far from having such a thought, having found him one of the greatest servants that God has on earth. If God does not permit his innocence to be recognized during his lifetime, one will be astonished to see in eternity the immense weight of the glory achieved by his suffering.

I again found a way to send this copy to the same person and asked him to keep it for me because it will always be easy to see from this copy the falseness of the original. And I have learned since that this person still has it.

My first thought was to go put myself in the Conciergerie and to present my complaint to Parliament, considering that it was a criminal matter. But besides the fact that I could only escape this house by implicating others in my affairs, it seemed to me that by doing this through a *lettre de cachet* [2] I would thus give them a hold on me with which they would not miss the chance to make another accusation against me, more founded than the others. I therefore remained in peace, waiting until it pleased God to arrange this, but counting on the greatest violence.

I knew through this good peasant that Monsieur de Cambrai asked unceasingly how I looked and what I said, but God did not permit that the least change or the least chagrin might be seen on my face or in my speech. I noticed that the girls would observe me attentively and would even appear troubled, but I acted in my ordinary way, treating them with the same politeness and keeping my profound silence. One skillfully proposed to me that I flee to avoid the bad treatment to which I was going to be exposed. But the trap was glaring; I was very far from doing this because it would have given my enemies an advantage.

With Desgrez being sick, I stayed in this situation for three weeks. Finally, having recovered at the end of that period of time, he came and told me that he had been strongly urged to come quickly and explained what had prevented him from doing so. He added that I had been accused of having committed a thousand crimes in this house. With this good country woman finding herself there at that moment, I asked her before him what I had done. "Alas, Madame," she responded, "nothing except good and not a single bad thing." I said to Desgrez: "You know what I told you while coming here—that I was only being brought here to make accusations about me. And see, this has proven quite true." He told me in a low voice and nearly with a tear in his eye: "What pity I feel for you." He had the order not to leave any paper without taking it. The parish priest thought to take back his letters by this order, but nothing was found. After sending me some things, one day, that I had asked him to have bought for me—they were books—horrible writings were found inside. I might never have taken care of this if, in wanting to unwind a skein, I had not noticed something terrible on the paper. I burned all of these papers. Whether he had given this order by design or this happened by chance, God only knows, but he had the goodness to help me in this as in all the rest.

It is necessary for me to talk about the disposition of my heart and all the sacrifices that God had me make in this house in Vaugirard. First, in spite of the storms there, I was in a state of very great tranquility, waiting from one moment to the next for the order of providence, to which I am devoted without reserve. My heart was continually sacrificed without sacrifice, happy to be the victim of providence.

One day—I was not thinking about anything—it was necessary for me to get on my knees and prostrate myself with a certainty that my girls would be taken from me so as to torment me further, and so as to torment them to force them to say something against me. I said this to them. They cried bitterly and begged me to ask God not to let this happen. Far from asking for that, I made a sacrifice of it, only being able to want God's will.

Another time, I had the premonition that communion would be taken away from me. It was necessary to sacrifice myself to this and to consent to communicate only with the will of God. All this happened.

After Desgrez had searched everywhere, he told me that I had to go to prison alone, without my girls. I offered no resistance and gave no sign of chagrin. They were desperate when they saw themselves torn from me. I told them that one must cling to nothing and that God would be everything for them. I left this way after having seen them being put violently into two separate carriages so that they would not know where they were taken. They were always separated, and what they were made to endure to make them speak out against their mistress goes beyond imagination, although God did not permit such torments to make them betray the truth. One of them is still in pain ten years later for having talked about the story of the poisoned wine before the judge. The other, whose mind was weaker, lost it through the excess and the length of such suffering, without their being able to draw one word against me out of her, even in her madness. She has been freed since then and returned to her parents. The good treatment that she was given and the care that her family provided her have brought her completely back, and now she lives there in peace serving God with all her heart.

I was then taken alone to the Bastille.

I forgot to say that since I had a dangerously high fever, I almost continuously took wine containing quinine. They were going to fetch some wine from the wine shop. Thus, whereas one glass of wine per day would normally be enough, all the other wine necessary for taking the quinine, joined with the normal amount I would take, made for a lot in a short time. They wrote about all this wine in the report, and, having shown it to Monsieur de Paris, it seemed to him that I was drinking about two pints per day because they had not put down that it was for the cinchona.[3] For this reason he reproached me for gorging myself on wine and meat. I still had such great stomach pain that I could not eat. I answered him that I was sure that if he saw me eat, he would find that I ate too little rather than too much. He asked if I had fasted during all of Lent. He was told yes. He made a disdainful face at that. He is certain that I was hardly in a state to do this, vomiting nearly all that I ate. However, I fasted for all of Lent with inexplicable pains. It was sometimes necessary to get up at night to get a little wine from Alicante; I thought I was dying.

After this wine had been taken away from me, the sister about whom I spoke came to talk to me about this and about others of the community of

Paris, so that I might say something that they could use against me. For with the wine being no more, all proof was missing. But I answered nothing. The parish priest even had the nerve to say in his letter and in his memoirs that, with my being unsatisfied with the best wine from Paris at one hundred ecus, I sent for even more to be taken from the wine shop. This wine was so poison-ous that, having taken a bottle to the Bastille to defend myself and to serve as evidence of what had happened at Vaugirard, a young woman, when sweeping away a spider web, caused this bottle to fall and break. The odor alone made her sick, and it took her some time to come out of it. She died shortly thereafter.

I cannot say all that happened to me in this house in great detail. All I can say is that I would have considered it a pleasure to go to the Bastille, if I had been allowed to keep my girls, or at least one of them, because I believed that I would only have to answer to Monsieur de La Reynie, who, being a righteous man full of honor, would not let me live in fear of any surprises. And as I told them, I fear nothing from the truth, but only from accusations and lies.

6

The Bastille

I WAS THUS put alone in a bare room in the Bastille. I arrived there on the eve of the little feast of God.[1] I sat down on the floor at first. Monsieur de Loncas [du Junca][2] loaned me a chair and a camping bed until my furniture arrived. This lasted four or five days, after which it was furnished. I was alone with an inexplicable happiness. But this did not last because I was given a young woman who, being of noble status but without wealth, hoped to make her fortune, as she had been promised, if she could find something against me. I felt the pain of being kept under watch, not because I feared it, but because I lost these happy moments when, being alone with my dear Master, nothing distracted me from him, and I do not see any happiness like that of being alone.

Since among my furniture from Vaugirard they brought me a lot of books like the Holy Scripture and other good books, they went to say at the Court that a cartload of books had been brought; they were said to be very bad books, and they ordered that an inventory be made. Monsieur du Junca had them taken, and, having found a secretary, they made an inventory. They were surprised to see that there were only good books. They found little pieces of divine love poetry there. They put on the inventory: "Emblems of Love."[3] I said to Monsieur du Junca: "Then finish what is after that." He had trouble doing this. The inventory was taken to Monsieur de Paris who, seeing nothing worse than what had been made known to the Court, did not send the inventory, being content that the Court had been persuaded that I had abominable books.

I had to suffer a lot at first, as much from the harshness that I was shown as from the humidity of the place, where for a long time there was no fire, which caused me to become very ill. I could not help myself into my bed. It was like a fainting spell that lasted almost twenty-four hours. They believed that I was going to die. I came out of it a little, and I asked Monsieur du Junca, who was there with the turnkey, to tell Monsieur de Paris that I was innocent of the things of which I was being accused, and that I protested this at my death. The turnkey, who was a very honest man, said: "I truly believe it, poor woman." I could not talk again until a long time later, but I quite clearly heard Monsieur du Junca tell him: "If you speak of this, you will have no executioner other than me." As soon as I was able to speak, I asked for confession. Father Martinot [Martineau] came for the first time.

I did not know him. I confessed to him with a fair amount of pain. When I started to do this, he sent for a doctor who was below. I was surprised to see that he did not finish hearing my confession. He came back with the doctor. He asked him if I was going to die at that moment. The doctor responded no, unless some new accident should happen. Then Father Martineau told me: "I have no power to hear your confession unless you are going to die soon." I told him that if I was overcome with new fainting spells I would not be in a condition to confess, and I would therefore die without confession. He had heard most of it. He left without wanting to hear me, saying that he had been forbidden to hear my confession, and that if I died, since that depended neither on him or me, I would be in peace. I do not know if these are his words, but this is the gist of it. And the same speech has been repeated to me several times. I was truly strongly in peace, having nothing that troubled me from this side, and having put my fate in the hands of God.

I still had this woman who spied on my words and everything else, supposing to make her fortune by doing this. One of my women sent me, through Desgrez, a stitched bonnet that she had made. This woman ripped it up. There was a note written in her blood, with her having no ink, and she let me know that she promised me, in a little piece of it that I found there still, that she would always be mine in spite of what they could do to her. She took it and gave it all to Monsieur du Junca.

As soon as I was able to keep myself in a chair, Monsieur d'Argenson⁴ came to interrogate me. He was so prejudiced and had so much fury that I had never seen anything like it. For it is necessary to notice that, it being apparent that Monsieur de La Reynie had treated me justly, he had been given another job and his had fallen to this man here, who was connected in every way to the people who persecuted me. I had resolved not to answer anything. Since he saw in effect that I was making no replies, he became furiously angry and told me that he had an order from the King to make me answer. I believed that it was better to obey. I answered. I believed, in spite of his accusations, that he would at least write down things as I had told him. I had seen such probity and good faith in Monsieur de La Reynie that I believed others to be the same.

Although I was very weak, an interrogation of eight hours was begun about what I had done since the age of fifteen, whom I had seen and who had served me. These three points were the subject of more than twenty interrogations, each one lasting several hours. I avow that I lacked my wits on this occasion, God permitting this without a doubt so as to make me suffer greatly. For nothing made me suffer as much as these interrogations in which, confident of speaking the truth, I spoke it, but I was afraid of not speaking it perfectly due to a fault of memory. The mean twists that they gave to everything and to the most accurate responses, never rendering them with my words or with my meaning, are things that cannot be expressed. I only had to say that, having been interrogated by Monsieur de La Reynie, I had nothing more to say in response to all these things, and that if I had done something since Vincennes, they only had to make it known, but I only dared to do that after it was too late. Moreover, since they still flattered themselves, and they did not believe their malice to be great enough as it was, I was persuaded that they wanted to acquire information by presenting formal charges and allowing me to plead my case, as I had requested in the first place. And I was sure that a procedure of this nature would have made my innocence apparent to the whole world. But they were very far away from that.

There were false letters in which my writing was so well forged that I would have had a lot of trouble recognizing it myself if, apart from the difference in style, they did not have me writing from places where I had never been and to people whom I had never met. Therefore, in order not to fall into this error, they wanted to assure themselves of the places that had been designated. [I said] that I had not changed the girls who were with me, and that as for the other matters, this had depended on the circumstances, and that, lackeys always having been responsible for these things, I could not remember them. Or something approaching this.

They moved from there into what they wanted, which was my widowhood. I answered with the truth, item by item, including the subject of my voyage to Gex, as well as the one that I took with Father La Combe, when I had taken a former monk along to accompany us. They did not want to put any of that down. They always made it seem as though I had been alone with him. In a trip that I took from Thonon to Geneva, which was only three leagues, we were a group of five or six. He never wanted to put it down that way and had it written: "She was with him in Geneva." Whatever I would say would be passed right over. I was shown the order of the King—false or true?—to treat me without any justice at all.

He himself put down one time, speaking of something that had happened at Monsieur Fouquet's home, that I did not yet live there at that time. I told him that I had never lived there and that such must not be stated. He told me:

"I have to interrogate you about this tomorrow, and I will put it down then." Since I did not penetrate all of his malice at that time, I believed him and signed. The next day I told him to put down that I had never lived in Monsieur Fouquet's home. He did not want to do any such thing.

It is necessary to know that at Monsieur Fouquet's home a relative of Madame his wife had been married to a man who had two wives, which made quite a stir. He was put in prison. This relative injured herself, and since she gave birth prematurely due to a great fall and there was a lawsuit against this crafty and malicious man, it was necessary to care for the child for six weeks until the end of the nine month term. He was baptized at St. Germain and died at the end of that time. They knew this story from the priest. Since they took advantage of all these stories, and they exaggerated the accounts of it for Rome and the people of the Court, they had started a rumor about this affair implicating me, without my knowing about it. And to make it more colorful, they had included the claim that I was not yet at the home of Monsieur Fouquet, so that it would appear that I had been there later and precisely at the time of this birth. Several other things happened to me of this nature that indicated the malice and the bad faith of Monsieur d'Argenson.

He asked me then how many times I had seen Monsieur de Cambrai. I told him: "I have never been to his home. He came to my home by order of Monsieur de Meaux"—which was true—"and never alone." When he came there on behalf of Monsieur de Meaux, it was for some business with St. Cyr. He put down that Monsieur de Cambrai had come three times to my home, and never wanted to put down, "by order of Monsieur de Meaux," even getting angry that I might pronounce his name, as if I had profaned it. When Monsieur de Cambrai was in question, he got furious. I told him, "Monsieur, a judge must not be so partial and show so much anger against the people whom he interrogates or against those that he wants to discuss during the interrogation, and show such devotion to the accusers' side." He became quite angry, and then he was no longer the lion but the fox.

Sometimes he would get angry at the responses that I gave him and say that I was being given advice. They looked everywhere to see if this was possible. A trellis of brass wire was placed over the chimney so, as they said, no written advice could be thrown through the opening. I told them, since it was true, that I had never been given advice, and that I had been guarded, that my room was visible from all sides, and that my tower was very high. He told me: "It is thus an angel who dictates your responses to you!" He said that with so much anger and scorn that fair people who would have seen him would have considered him incapable of being a judge in an affair where he showed so much passion. Under this foot of prejudice and of anger he crushed all my responses, without hearing the least little bit I was saying.

One day, as he was going on, the clerk, picking up his papers to put them back in his case, said to me in a whisper: "Poor woman, how you arouse my pity!" He noticed that I had stayed near the clerk. I spoke aloud about some meaningless thing. He fixed a frightening stare upon him and did not stop at all until he had left the room. From that time on the clerk did not dare to look at me.

I swear that if I had been able to guess the treatment that Monsieur d'Argenson was going to give me, so different from that of Monsieur de La Reynie, I would never have responded to him. But the fear of wronging others by not responding made me break the silence that I had resolved to keep. I suffered from a very strange oppression, caused by a clever and malicious judge who had prepared his ready materials in writing, and who gave a violent twist to my responses, trying to insert his venom. Me, without defense or counsel, observed on all sides, mistreated in all ways, whom they tried to intimidate in every fashion.

After he put down that I had not remained there, at Monsieur Fouquet's home, Monsieur du Junca came to talk to me about the priest at St. Germain as a man who was his friend and who knew a lot about my news. Since Monsieur Fouquet and his relative had confided everything to me, I understood why Monsieur d'Argenson had put that down in my response, and I saw all the enmity. Then the governor⁵ and Monsieur du Junca would direct severe and frightening looks toward me, but all this did not frighten me. The best defense is innocence and confidence.

After this interrogation, which was so long that it lasted nearly three months—and great criminals had never been given such long ones—they took two years, apparently to get information from everywhere. They asked the woman who was with me if I did not speak against religion and if I did not commit crimes. She told them that I was very far from this, that I was full of sweetness and patience, that I prayed to God and read good books, and that I consoled her because she was in a horrible despair, the cause of which I will explain.

She was a noble woman, but very poor, responsible for three children. She found a bourgeois man from Paris, very rich, who wanted to marry her, and who would have given his wealth to her children or to her, if she had none. They had made him believe that she had to live in the company of a lady in a convent and that she would see whomever she pleased. They said that it was only for three months and that she would even leave for her business. However, they pressured her to come to the Bastille in order to speak to Monsieur du Junca.

When she came, they made her go up into a room and closed her up with me. She was there for several days without getting upset, believing that she would be leaving to put her affairs in order. But when she saw that they did not want to let her leave or talk to anyone, she fell into horrible despair. She took it out on me and told me what fury inspired her to say. I assured her that I had girls who had been taken from me by force, and who would have been very happy to be able to spend their lives with me in prison, and that she had been given to me by force, in the same way that they were retaining her there. She was a bit appeased. She was even promised a great fortune if she could say something against me.

Although she was a Thiange on her mother's side, and of a rather good house on her father's side, being the cousin—or niece, rather—in the line of Brittany of Madame la Maréchale de La Motte, she had been raised with so little religion that she did not know the first principles that children learn while young, and she thought but little about God. Everything seemed permissible to her. She was not capable of being touched by any feeling for God. And since, at first, what I could say to console her was suspect from her perspective due to the bad impression of me that she had been given, she believed that a woman can have a marriage consistent with her conscience with an already married man and that it sufficed to promise faithfulness to each other to be legitimately married, although the man might have another woman. I took all the trouble imaginable to disabuse her of this.

She believed that it was permissible to take everything from me. She cut my sheets and took possession of everything that I had because I was in prison. Despite my pains and a great illness that I had from the torments of Monsieur d'Argenson, I was occupied all day in trying to prevent her from falling into despair. I did not dare to appear sad or even recollected in front of her. They would have believed that my sadness was proof of my crime, and the recollecting would have been another, very terrible one. I was thus observed in all ways. I attest that this was no small torment.

However, this woman was sometimes touched by acts of kindness that I did for her and by my sweetness. But since they threatened her once or twice a week, for several hours, in a place where she was interrogated with all sorts of promises and where they said that I was a hypocrite or a heretic, when she would return from these conversations in the chamber below mine, she would look at me with astonishment and horror. When she had not spoken to them for a few days, she would show esteem for me, but this did not end her despair.

Finally, she became sick from chagrin. It was a continuous, very violent fever and an inflammation of the chest. She appeared very sick at first. I asked Monsieur du Junca to have her given confession. He did not want this at all. She was in extreme need, for I saw that she was at death's door. I took more care of her than a servant takes of her mistress. Being alone with her, I spent seven nights without changing clothes or going to bed. It was often necessary to empty her basins. I did everything with an open heart, but without strength. I spoke to her about God as much as I could.

One night when I found her very sick, I had her recite the act of contrition. With tears, she promised God no longer to fall into her sins if she got over it. As soon as I was no longer with her, she imagined that the Devil would enter and remain so close to her bed that she would call out for me in a horrible fright. I would go to her with holy water. As soon as I would appear, she would say: "He disappeared." Since I saw the state she was in, I begged Monsieur du Junca with much insistence to let her make a confession. He told me with a frightening air . . . [*his response is missing*]. That night, she was very sick. I did what I could to help her along. The next morning, not being able to do any more, I went to bed. She called out to me: "Madame, come quickly!" I only had time to get out of bed and put on my slippers. She told me: "There is no more time. I am his. It is done. I am damned." I did what I could to console her.

Due to the care that I took of her, what I told her, and the harshness of the others' not wanting to let her make a confession, and with her not seeing the doctor or the surgeon who had come to bleed her, she was feeling great esteem for me and said: "Since I am damned, I must not be in your room." Since I had made it known that she was very ill, the surgeon came with Monsieur du Junca. She said: "Let them take me away. I am damned." They believed themselves to have made a lucky discovery,[6] and that she meant to say that they should take her out of my room because I had damned her. This was the opposite of what she was saying—that since she was damned, she must not stay in my room.

. They took witnesses about what she said. They had the doctor come, to whom she said the same thing. They believed themselves to elicit a lot of things against me from her. They came to take her away that night and made her go to the chaplain at the Bastille. She had asked for the priest or the vicar from St. Côme, but they did not want to have him come. They hoped that the chaplain would get a lot of things out of her against me and that the testimony of a dying person could have great weight. But as she was losing consciousness, she told them good about me, and, not wanting to have the chaplain hear her confession, she still asked for her confessor. Since she had confided her sins to me that night, I was very afflicted to see her die without confession, in the state she was in. But since they refused her request for her confessor, she ended up going into an absolute delirium. Her illness was an inflammation of the chest, for which one never bleeds the foot. However, due to their desire to get something out of her about me, sparing nothing and wishing only to hurt me, they drew blood from her foot twice in succession, which caused her to die without regaining consciousness.

Since they wanted to use what they claimed to have gotten out of this woman against me, in one way or another—the thing having passed them by—they talked about it with Father Martineau, who came to see me every now and again, with a view toward his telling me that this woman had made some strong depositions against me. This father, who believed this in good faith and who penetrated nothing beyond that, communicated this to me the first time that I saw him. I did not appear at all surprised to him since, indeed, I was not. For no longer being capable of making things up, I feared nothing from the truth, but everything from lies. This father told me that the testimony of a dying person was very strong.

Monsieur d'Argenson came with an even more severe air than ordinary. He told me that this woman said many things against me, implying that she was still alive and in a state to confront me. Since I was frank, I responded to him that she was dead. He replied to me: "How do you know that?" I told him that I did not doubt it, although I had not actually been told. Since he believed that someone had told me about it, he said that he was referring to what she had been able to declare while dying. I told him that she had left my room delirious. When he saw that I was not going along with him, he once again began to interrogate me and sought other things to interrogate me about regarding this woman, and my responses could have been written, but God did not permit it.

It seemed that God was putting himself on the side of the men during this time because I was strongly coerced, both on the inside and the outside.[7] Everything was against me. I saw all men united to torment me and to surprise me—all the artifice and all the subtlety of the minds of people who have much of these—who worked together against me on this. And I was alone, without recourse, feeling on me the weight of the heavy hand of God, who seemed to abandon me to myself and to my own obscurity, an entire desertion within. I was unable to help myself with my natural mind, in which all vivacity had been deadened for such a long time, since I had ceased to use it in order to let myself be led by a superior mind, having worked all my life to submit my mind to Jesus Christ and my reason to his guidance. But in all this time I could not help myself, either with my reason or with any interior support, because I was like those who have never felt this admirable guidance from God's kindness and who have no natural mind. When I prayed, I only had responses of death. At this time this passage of David came to me: *When they persecute me, I aggrieved my soul through fasting* (Ps. 35:13). I therefore practiced very rigorous fasting and austere penances for as long as my health would permit, but this seemed like burning straw to me. And one moment of God's guidance is one thousand times more help.

They gave me another girl who was Monsieur du Junca's goddaughter. He went so far as to imply that he would marry her so that he would be able to get more information out of her than he otherwise could have. And he gave her the strongest evidence of passion. Since she was only nineteen years old, and he was persuaded that there was nothing that one would not do for those by whom one is loved, he believed himself to have found a sure means to succeed in his designs and to earn merit for himself among the people who were persecuting me. I believe that he would have had consideration for me without this great desire that he had to please them. He did not conceal this from me and would tell me that, owing his fortune to the Messieurs de Noailles, there was nothing that he would not do for them. He said that they had promised that he would be the governor of the Bastille and that they had not been able to avoid appointing Monsieur de Saint-Mars, but that he was going to die and, therefore, M. du Junca was only taking a step back so that he could jump higher. I knew in my heart that he would never be governor of the Bastille, and without explaining myself, I told him that often the oldest outlived the youngest. However, they would always send the new information that they fabricated about me to Rome, and, provided that they were able to give some color to the calumny through artifice, that was enough.

On the one hand, Father Martineau told me the most outrageous things, even insults, as if I was the worst wretch of them all. But I saw that he was doing violence to himself, and that, being naturally honest, he was only following the instructions that he had been given. Two or three days after having said all of these incredible, harsh things to me, which I received with as much sweetness and tranquility as if he had told me the most obliging things in the world, he told me that he did not insult me voluntarily, but that he was obligated to obey. On the other hand, Monsieur du Junca, who knew nothing except that he believed me to be an outrageous heretic and a despicable person, said all the harsh things imaginable to me. He could not reconcile all of my tranquility and gaiety with all of my difficulties. He attributed everything to my malice because they had prejudiced him. They were all in despair that I did not give them any hold over me by exhibiting fits of anger or by some word on which they could rely to torment me once more. But although my natural state was quick tempered, God did not permit this.

When the trial in Rome was lost,[8] they all celebrated, and it was then that for several days they, and Father Martineau, stopped insulting me. I always remained the same. They came to ask me what I thought Monsieur de Cambrai would do after this. I responded: "He will submit; he is too righteous to do otherwise." They believed without a doubt that I would say that an injustice had been done to him, and that, having shown more force in supporting him than myself, I would display extreme chagrin and a fit of anger. But they saw the same equanimity toward this as toward the rest. They asked this young woman whom they had put with me if I was not truly sad. She responded no. When they had finished with all of their intrigues, Monsieur du Junca came on behalf of Monsieur de Paris to tell me that there were sometimes reasons one was obligated to do things that one would not want to do, and that if I should write a letter of apology to Monsieur de Paris and ask him to come to see me, I would be released. I believe that he was speaking in good faith, and that I might perhaps have been released at that time. But I was so accustomed to seeing myself taken in by tricks that I did not doubt that this was one of them, and they wanted me to sign Monsieur de Cambrai's condemnation. I responded to this that I had nothing to ask Monsieur de Paris and still less to tell him, and that, as such, it would be truly useless to ask him to come here. I said that I did not desire to leave, and that I was fine in my solitude. They no longer spoke about this to me. I was truly resolved, if they had wanted to make me sign this condemnation, to say that it was not for women to condemn bishops, and that I submitted to the decision of the Pope, just as he had submitted to it.

Perhaps it will be thought that, after so many interrogations and my having been presented with a forged letter from Father La Combe, which had caused such a stir in the world, they would have shown me the letters again and interrogated me about this. I waited for this and even desired it. But they did not speak to me about it at all. However, they spread the rumor that I had been confronted about it. I would have desired this, but how to confront a man who only said good about me and who never thought to write me the letters that were attributed to him? They did not find a way to put this into play other than to interrogate me about my whole life—where had I been, whom had I seen, who had given me confession, and things of this nature. But they never spoke to me in the interrogations other than to ask questions such as,

"Who accompanied you to such and such a place?" I said that it was him, along with another elderly priest, and that there were six of us. They only wanted to write him and me down, and they said that the chance for speaking about it would come, and that what I wanted would be written down.

Soon after the affair had been judged in Rome, they stopped interrogating me, but they did not allow me confession. They strongly urged me to say that I did not want Father Martineau. I was made to think that his refusal to hear my confession was against Monsieur de Paris's intention, and that if I asked the chaplain, he would hear my confession and offer me communion first. Father Martineau, on his side, assured me that he had been forbidden to do this. It is incredible all the promises and the threats that were used to have me take as my confessor the chaplain of the Bastille, an unknown provincial man. For I had always said that, since Monsieur de Paris had given me Father Martineau, whom I did not know before, he could have given him permission to hear my confession, that I did not know who the chaplain was, that I had already experienced what comes from the desire for profits, and that it would be easy to convince others that I had sworn a lot of things to this man about which I had never thought. I had also said that a man from a well-known order had his own honor and that of his order to preserve, and that I believed him incapable of invention, that as such I would go to him and not to others, and that he could confess me as well as another. Moreover, he would garner no profits. When afterwards he was declared to be the confessor of princes, they came to find me and told me that this was worth a benefit, and that apparently I would leave him right away. They explained to me all the evil that he could do to me.

What is surprising is that Father Martineau, on his side, treated me harshly. However, I never wanted to leave him, and I persevered until the end. If I had been alone in this affair, my God knows well that I would not have taken so many precautions and that I would have done what they wanted. But since I considered that I was obligated to consecrate myself to God and to offended piety, the Devil putting forth all his efforts and causing contemplative people to be accused so as to discredit them, and that I was obligated to consecrate myself to my friends and to my family (which was the least of my worries), I did not want anyone to be able to say that I had sworn a single lie.

I believe that it will not be bad here to make a little related digression. From the beginning of the world, the Devil has always aped God. He has behaved this way throughout time. And when St. Peter made such great miracles, Simon the Magician tried very hard to imitate him and even to surpass him (Acts 8:9-24). Afterward, St. Clement of Alexandria showed that just as there were true Gnostics, admirable men, there were false ones who brought about abominations. In the time of St. Theresa, who was truly inspired by God, wretched visionaries, inspired by the Devil, gained prominence in Spain. In this century, when there are simple people who are truly interior and contemplative, miserable creatures under the guidance of a certain Father V[autier] have arisen, and elsewhere in another manner, so that their abominations, being discovered, disparaged the ways of the Lord and caused the persecution of those who were the most opposed to them. I wrote several letters before being put in prison and before I was tormented, which showed how much I accused them and put people on guard against them. I have living witnesses of this, and thus I alerted all sides to be suspicious of them; I have believed this digression useful.

7

The Abyss

TO RETURN TO the Bastille, I thus had the goddaughter of Monsieur du Junca around me, with the promise that he had made to marry her. He thought that he might draw all that he wanted against me from her. Such an awful portrait of me had been made for her that she trembled to come. She feared, she told me, that I was going to strangle her at night. He promised that she would only be there for as long as she found it suitable. He assured her, nonetheless, that I was sweet and that I would not harm her.

She came dressed in a coquettish manner, displayed both by her hairstyle and by showing her throat. She was very pretty. She had been raised with enough fear of God. I did not speak to her at first about hiding her throat or letting down her hair. I left her free. However cautioned she had been against me, she was not with me for one week before she considered me a friend through any kind of trial and also had a proportionate confidence in me. She saw that I often prayed to God.

Since she had been in a convent for a long time and she knew that contemplative prayer was performed, she asked me how to do it properly. I gave her some places in the Passion on which to meditate. She profited so much by this that on her own she began to hide her throat carefully and to wear her hair modestly. She had such an extreme fear of death that when she read me something, she passed over the word "death" without reading it and asked me not to speak of it. During the first days, prejudiced by what she had been told, she pulled my hair while combing it, making me turn my head with blows from her fists. But then, although she was very quick tempered, if it had been necessary for her to give her blood for me, she would have done it. I believe that the patience that God gave me to tolerate all that she did to me contributed in no small measure to her conversion.

After she had been with me for a little while, she let me speak to her about death. I saw that she was mortifying herself in everything. When she had already decided to put on something that was very becoming and wear it to Sunday mass, after halfway putting it on, she would have an impulse to put on something less becoming and go with that. I saw her mortifying herself, and she would tell me after it was done that she had been as apprehensive about prison and death as she was ecstatic to be there now. She was led to ask God to let her die near me and never return again into the world. She asked this in spite of the repugnancies in her nature, which were so extreme that she became sick. In the same measure as she overcame such things, the ability to perform contemplative prayer was given to her, and her contemplative prayer became simpler, with an ability to recollect.

After she had broken a certain bottle of wine from Vaugirard, of which I have already spoken,[1] she fell ill. She told me once about how Monsieur de... had wanted terrible things from her and about the resistance that she had shown him. He was listening at the door. He entered at that moment, quite forbidden. I saw clearly that he had heard everything, and I was pained by it. He has shown such an aversion toward her since then that, if she had consented to it, he would have had her leave immediately. He brought an apothecary who was very devoted to him, and, being a man without religion, he wanted, in spite of me, to give her a pill himself, which he said only consisted of cassia and would prevent her from becoming sick. From the moment she took it, there was no more hope for her life. Her fever, which had been recurring and slight, became continual, her face changed, and he assured himself that she would never recover.

For her part, she asked God, in spite of herself, for her to die from this illness. They wanted her to leave to get fresh air. After first opposing this, she would only leave on the condition that she would be brought back to me again. They promised her this, knowing that she would not return. She told me: "If I believed that I was dying, I would not leave so as to die near you." They were in despair that the plans they had developed to make her share their views and interests had gone so badly. Her extreme youth had made them believe that she would succumb to all the promises of fortune that they continually put before her eyes, and that she would say all that they wanted against me due to that. But when they saw the opposite and how firm she was in upholding my interests, they only wanted to get her away from me from then on. I gave her all the care imaginable night and day for four months. Finally, she was taken away while she was with me.

They used her confession to inspire bad sentiments against me in her. But what she saw was so contrary to what she had been told that she upheld the truth with courage beyond her years. She was told to take care to avoid my corrupting her, and since she felt the mercies that God had given her since she was with me, she cried bitterly from the stubbornness of these people. She counted on staying near me for as long as she lived, but after she had stayed there, in the same room, for three years, it was necessary for her to go. She died two weeks later, having become emaciated.

I did not want to have any more people around me. I stayed alone for one and a half years. I had a fever for one year, without saying anything about it.[2] I was alone for more than a year because, the young lady of whom I have spoken having died, I asked that no more of them be given to me under the pretext that they would die. Thus, I spent the days and nearly all the nights without sleeping because I only went to bed after midnight and got up at the light of day. I developed a sickness in my eyes such that I could not read or work, and although I was very deserted on the inside, I was happy without happiness from the will of God.

As soon as this girl of whom I just spoke had died, they came to speak to me. I believed myself to have made the mercies of God known to this poor child. God took her from the world at the age of twenty-one so that she would not be corrupted by it later, for they no longer wanted her to be with me and were about to return her to it.

To return to what concerned me, Monsieur d'Argenson, after having gone two years without interrogating me, and after having interrogated me for such a long time, as I have said, came back after all that time.

Above my room there was a prisoner who had been brought there. It seemed as though this man was guilty because he walked night and day without ceasing, without resting for one moment, and ran around like a maniac. One St. Bartholomew's Day, when we were getting ready for mass, we heard him fall, and then we did not hear anything else. After the mass, we were taken to dinner. I told this young lady: "Go listen at the door when dinner is carried up there, for I fear this man might have harmed himself." Actually, when they opened the door, they cried out: "Go fetch a surgeon and Monsieur du Junca!" The man was drowning in his own blood. He had opened up his chest. They dressed his wound with such care that he was healed after eight or ten months. They sewed him up and claimed that it was one of the most admirable cures that had ever been provided. If he had done this at night, he would have been found dead.

Such things often happen in places like these, and I am not surprised by them. Only the love of God, abandonment to his will, and conformity to the suffering of Jesus Christ, joined with innocence, allow one to live in such a place in peace, without which the harshness that is experienced there without consolation throws one into despair. You are made to experience only what can bring you pain in this place and nothing that can bring you pleasure. You only see terrible faces, which only treat you most harshly. You are without defense when you are accused. They circulate rumors on the outside as they want. In other prisons you have counsel if you are accused; you have lawyers in order to defend yourself and judges who, in examining the truth, enlighten one another. But here, you have no one. You have only one judge, who is most often judge and jury, as has happened to me, who interrogates you as he pleases, who writes down whatever he wants from your answers, and who is free from all rules of justice, and there is no one at all who corrects him afterwards. They try to persuade you that you are guilty; they make you believe that there are a lot of things against you. And the poor people who do not know what faith in God or abandonment to his will are, and who moreover feel guilty, grow desperate.

Getting back to Monsieur d'Argenson, he returned after two years, no longer with his furious air but in a sheep's clothing, so as to make me fall more easily into the trap that he had designed for me. I have never been offered such politeness and such care as he offered me. However, since nothing had been found against me up to then, they believed themselves to have found a way to justify all their past violence with the man who had split his chest open above my room. He was a priest. I have never known why he was there. All that I know is that he said that he saw me at the Ursulines in Thonon and that if they would save his life, he would say everything against me that they wanted. It was necessary that he be fit to appear. They made up his interrogation as they wanted it, and he signed it.

He submitted first that, since I had been very sick, Father La Combe brought me the good God, and that he stayed without returning home for more than three hours. This could have been true because he said mass for the nuns and heard their confessions.

It is remarkable to note that until now, during such a great multitude of interrogations that had been conducted with me, I have not yet been accused of anything, and they only wanted to know what I had said, seen, and done since the age of fifteen and where I had been. Monsieur de La Reynie had only interrogated me about letters, as I have said. The clergymen had only done so about my books. But then, these are a form of accusation. I will say what I remember about them.

They interrogated me about a notebook with Father La Combe's handwriting, which the priest said he had seen, in which he had read the following passage: "Oh, happy sin that brings us such great advantages." And there were also some other words that I do not remember. I said that I had no idea about this, but that in any case, these were pious writings in which he had put down what the Church sings: "*O felix culpa.*"[3] He never wanted to put down my response and said that this signified something else. He put simply that I did not remember, without putting down "*O felix culpa,*" which was the meaning of these words.

Then he told me that the priest accused me of having written him a lot of letters containing things that were not good. I responded that I did not remember ever seeing him, that I remembered still less ever having written to him, that if he had my letters, he needed only to produce them, and that I would never disavow my own handwriting. They put down my response.

I was again told what this man had submitted—because the depositions were being read such as they had been written—that I was a thief, a godless woman, a blasphemer, an indecent woman, a person so cruel that I said that "I would chop my girl up like a flesh pâté"—these are his terms—"if I believed that God wanted it or if I got it in my head to do it." They did not specify any particular action to me that had any relationship whatsoever to these crimes, but only that I had said it.

This accusation gave me such joy in my depths that I could not express it, seeing myself, like you, my dear Master, in the ranks of criminals. I was free to show that when one leaves behind the wealth that I have left behind, it is not to take the wealth of others, that there was no place where I had lived in which the churches did not bear the marks of my piety, and that I had made no sermon in my whole life, which everyone knows. As for cruelty, there was never anyone further from it, for I could not kill a chicken. Besides, Monsieur de Paris, with a mocking air, had told me at Vaugirard that I had not been cruel to men, although this surely was a chapter in which God bestowed upon me more graces than I deserved, as one could see in the story of my *Life*. There was still the charge that I was dishonest and a liar. To all of that I made no response, except that it was necessary to show when and how I had committed these crimes.

Then he said that he had seen me in another place at the home of a priest playing *echets*; I said that I had never learned this game. They said that it was the game of pick-up sticks. They told me it was one place rather than another because this place was called something else. I said that I had not been to this place, and that I had stopped in another place while returning from Bourbon, but that the priest was not there and that it was not the place with the name they were giving.

They said that after this priest had come to see me there, I had acted as though I did not know him, and I had received him very poorly. Then they had me telling him confidential things so astonishing that if I had had such feelings, which I never would have, I would not have acted this way with my best friends. They had me speaking against the state, against M. de Meaux, to whom I had at that time a thousand obligations, and against my best friends. The conversation that they supposed me to have had with him was the subject of several interrogations. I defended myself as much as I could concerning the things about which they asked me, showing the implausibility of my speaking in this way about people for whom I had, even then, an infinite respect that I will retain for the rest of my life.

My excessive frankness caused me to laugh at a great fault because I had Monsieur d'Argenson in a place where he could offer no reply. Since he had himself taken this man's depositions, and he wrote down my responses as he pleased, he told me directly, without shame: "Oh, I am very happy with this interrogation; there is no longer refuge nor deceit!" Finally, I do not know what words made me understand that I would never escape from this. I had enough proof of his malicious prejudice to have to let him make all this happen without saying anything. But he told me, after so many interrogations, that, nonetheless, he still had to interrogate me the next day on this pretend conversation that he accused me of having.

And that interrogation had caused me pains about which God alone knows, because although I was prepared by the grace of God for any event, God permitting it to be so, I suffered from inexpressibly wrenching abdominal pains for the thirty-five or forty days that the interrogation lasted. And except for two or three times when they had me take a little wine, all this time I was not eating or sleeping, without it being possible to do otherwise and with God supporting me by laying his hand on me to keep me alive without eating.

I therefore said to Monsieur d'Argenson that I was very surprised that a man who said that I had given him such a chilly reception that I had pretended not to know him could brag that I had confided such strange things to him and said things that I would never imagine. For I declare before God that it was such astonishing doctrinal gibberish that after it had been read to me several times, it was impossible for me to understand anything and still less to draw the least meaning from it. I simply told him then, believing that he had written it, that it was not plausible that I would have shared such secrets with a man who complained of my incivility and my coldness. I said, moreover, that his deposition claimed that he had only spoken with me for one hour, but two days would not suffice to communicate so many things on subjects and topics of the kind they claimed I had discussed with him. And addressing him directly, I added: "How, sir, could a conversation lasting one hour, like the one he mentions in his deposition, be consistent with all that I am supposed to

have told him and with the things about which you have told me you still have
to interrogate me?"

He saw his blunder at once, but he never wanted to write down what I told
him, assuring me that the next day, at the end of his interrogation, he would
put down my reflections. I understood that it would be even more advantageous to me if they added eight hours to this supposed conversation. The
clerk said: "I have already included the remark that Madame made, but I must
not say anything." There was still a long document that needed to be completed for this interrogation, but profiting from my simplicity, he pretended
to have business at home, made me sign the interrogation, took his papers and
did not come back the next day as he had said he would. I clearly saw my fault
and the malice of my judge, but what was there to do except suffer what one
cannot prevent?

I believe that what motivated him to conduct this last interrogation, in
which they wanted at all costs to make a criminal out of me, is that in the Assembly of the Clergy in the year 1700, with Monsieur the Archbishop of Sens
presiding, they had made a declaration. While condemning my little book,
A Short and Easy Method, and my *Commentary on the Song of Songs,* they
declared that there had never been a question of morality concerning me, for
I had always shown great horror for all sorts of wickedness, as could be seen in
the findings of fact of this assembly, conducted and led under the eyes of
M. de Meaux, the most zealous of my persecutors. It appears that this declaration troubled them somewhat and that it made them involve the unhappy
priest about whom I heard no more after they confronted me with him.

After this last interrogation my difficulties became much worse. I saw only
frightening faces. I was treated like a criminal. They came to take from me
some letters from my children that someone had left. I had burned a few of
them. They threatened me, saying that I had better find them. Father Martineau redoubled his insults and his harsh treatment, due to orders he had
received. They only sent for me rarely, through the turnkey, for mass, or
through someone else of the same sort. Monsieur du Junca came no more,
which consoled me, because as I have said God's hand weighed me down on
the inside more than these men did on the outside. It was then that, seeing
that no form of justice was observed and that they had a miserable man say
everything that they wanted him to say, I believed that with things being
based only on lies, they would perhaps make me die. This thought gave me
such joy that I ate and slept. And when I wanted to distract myself, I would
dream of the pleasure that I would have in seeing myself on the scaffold.
I thought that maybe one would not want to make this injustice complete,

and that my grace would be seen on the scaffold. I thought that to prevent it I would tell the executioner to do his job the moment I climbed up there, and that grace only coming after the blow had been given, I would have the pleasure of dying for my dear Master.

I owe the young lady who was with me a lot because although she saw that I did not eat and I told her these things, she always claimed that I was in good spirits and content. It is true that when I saw someone, God would give me a face that was in good spirits and content. They would have liked to see me in despair and to see me in mortal sorrow, but they saw nothing of all that, because although I suffered a lot, I was not at all sorrowful. It was a completely interior suffering that was consuming me.

Finally, after a fair amount of time had passed, Monsieur d'Argenson returned. It was no longer a question of the priest's conversation; they no longer wanted to speak to me about that. This was about new things. This man had said that I had lodged with Father La Combe in one of the places I had been. I explained that I had lodged on the outskirts of the city, at the home of a Treasurer of France, and he had lodged at the home of a young woman at the other end of the city. He said that he had seen him at the home of Madame Languet, the widow of the General Procurer. This was true. He said that he saw me give him bullion. I said that I did this a lot for the poor, and that I had stayed that day to take care of him. I said yes to that, but that Madame Languet, M[ademois]elle her daughter and the D[emois]elle were also there, that we accompanied it with a little figure of Jesus made out of broken wax, that I had wanted to give him money to go to Rome so as to request a bishopric *in partibus* for the Father, and that I promised to give him three thousand pounds each year as a pension, in order to preserve his dignity. I said that I did not keep this promise, which I had not done because, having only two thousand eight hundred pounds of revenue, I could not give a thousand ecus, especially being obligated to live myself, barely having enough of what I needed for this.

Finally after many childish speeches, he told me that he would bring me the man so that I might confront him, and that I would make no mistake about who he was. I said that if I knew him, I would say so. He urged me not to get angry with this man, and from this I understood that he feared that I would intimidate him. A few days later they brought this man to me. It is necessary to note that they had started a rumor running all through Paris that I was being confronted with Father La Combe, and they never mentioned that he had written or said anything against me. They only mentioned his name to me incidentally.

They brought me the man whom I had trouble recognizing as a man of whose conduct I had already disapproved, for being disorderly. Without a doubt he was told this, but as I have said, I am still not sure of it. When I saw him, I said to him: "How, sir, can you accuse me of being a thief, etc.?" He said that he had not said this. I told Monsieur d'Argenson to have it written that he was recanting. I said that I was appealing to Parliament, that I was asking that the affair be taken away from its current jurisdiction, and that I protested the legal invalidity of all that had happened. Never have I seen such a furor as that of Monsieur d'Argenson. He threatened me by the King. I responded to him that the King would not find it a bad thing for me to defend my innocence before this sovereign Court, and that he was too fair-minded for that. He continued to read a book without listening to anything, but when it was at the place in the notebook of which I have spoken, the priest said: "Sir, it was *O felix culpa* that was there." I kept quiet, not wanting to respond after my protest because I did not want to take up any of this, but Monsieur d'Argenson, looking at him with a furious air, told him: "You are an idiot," and did not want to write these words: "*O felix culpa.*" When he asked me for my responses, I protested still the invalidity of the proceedings and said that I was appealing to Parliament. The man said nothing at all. And, however, they wrote that he persisted in his claims. They asked me if I wanted some witnesses. I said that I would tell Parliament my reasons for making legal challenges, and I continued to protest this invalidity. This being finished, this priest, trembling and pale as death, signed his name. I signed with a good heart in spite of the threats that they were making to me. I waited from one moment to the next for another scene. For Monsieur d'Argenson told me: "You are weary of being in an honorable prison. You want to taste the Conciergerie, and you will have a taste of it."

Sometimes, when going downstairs, I would be shown a door, and I would be told that the questioning was conducted there. At other times, I would be shown a cell; I would say that I found it very pretty, and I would like to stay there. They said that water leaked in there. I would tell them: "They only need to put a board under the arch and put my bed there, with a chair and a hatch for food. I would do very well there." They saw me always the same in spite of the threats. They got tired of making terrible faces at me, and they left me in peace. Monsieur d'Argenson appeared no more, although I believed that he could have shown up at any time.

But the appeal to Parliament was a clap of thunder; I fell ill. I was like this for more than a year. I hid my fever for over eight months. I was so happy to be alone that I would not have changed my fate even to be a queen. I had moments where I believed that I was going to die all alone.

One night, among others, when I was in the dressing room, I felt my life leaving me. I tried to get to my bed to die on it. This dressing room was a corner where I had put up some curtains, which served as a retreat in one of the archways of my chamber. But I did not die, God reserving other crosses for me. I was so excited to die this way, alone, since they would not give me confession, and I made it a pleasure to die alone with my dear Master, in the abandonment of all things. I had always hid my illnesses until extreme thinness together with the inability to stand on my legs caused me to be found out.

They sent for a doctor, who was a very honest man and gave me some remedies, although they were useless. The apothecary gave me some poisoned opium. I have come to know, since my release, who sent this. I refused it. I showed it to the doctor who told me, in my ear, not to take any of it at all and said that it was poison. This surgeon put some on his tongue, which swelled up right away. Getting wind of this, the apothecary, under the pretext of coming to see me, took the bottle on my table and, hiding it under his coat, left and took it away.

If someone reading this pays attention to the crosses that it pleased God to have me undergo, let him reflect on the care of his providence in delivering me from so many nearly inevitable dangers.

Before the last interrogation, I had two dreams. In the first, Father La Combe appeared to me affixed to a cross, just as I had seen in a dream more than twenty years earlier. But instead of the way he had seemed all brilliant and shining to me before, he appeared to me then hurt and deathly pale, his head wrapped up in a cloth. It seemed to me that he told me: "I am dead," and that he was encouraging me. I asked him how he was. "The sufferings of this life are not worthy to be compared to the glory that is prepared for us." And he added forcefully: "For a light suffering, one has the weight of an immense glory." I woke up.

I dreamed then that I found myself traveling down a path that was imperceptibly leading me into an oven where wood was being turned into coal, with boards all ablaze, covered with earth. I had made my way along much of the higher ground. And I saw a bigger pathway where flames appeared in a few places. This pathway forced me to descend. And I found a river at the bottom, so that I could only descend from the fire by going into the water, not seeing any other way out. There came a venerable lady who offered me her hand and made me enter into the church of Notre-Dame. I remembered this passage: "they have passed through fire and through water."[4]

The difficulty that I had was a woman who would come to clean my room. She had sometimes helped in the kitchen of Madame de B.,[5] where she had committed a theft. She took all I had from me. She had keys made from mine. Whatever I did, I could not prevent it. I did not dare to say anything because she was supported by the chaplain. I said something about it one day to this chaplain, who told me that everyone had their vices, that I had mine and that this was hers. He said that when she wanted to take something from me, I should give her ten or twenty ecus to prevent it. All my revenue would not have sufficed. I did not doubt that I had a spy. It was necessary to let her take everything without saying anything. On the other hand, they did not let the governor come to see me at all because it seemed that he had some esteem for me. They were all surprised by my sweetness and the patience that God gave me, and when I returned to my room from mass, I went up with joy.

The nephew of the governor said to me while taking me back that I was truly different from the others who fell into despair in their rooms. I answered him that I found what I loved there, and that maybe the others did not find that there. He was not rich; however, he helped prisoners as much as he could and had compassion for them. I told him one day that God would surely give him a better fortune. He attested to me that, only being able to have it at the cost of the governor's son's life, he would not want it. This son has since died, and he is naturally the governor's heir. Monsieur du Junca told me, in order to excuse himself for the pain that he had caused me, that he owed his fortune to Messieurs de Noailles, of whom his father had been a servant; that he would be the governor of the Bastille after the death of Monsieur de Saint-Mars; and that he already could smell the deal. I told him that younger people often die before older ones. I could not get away from the idea that he would die before the governor. He did in fact die before him. Of what use to him was this desire for fortune? And of what use was such prudence at the expense of charity and justice?

8

Deliverance

AFTER SEVEN OR eight months of illness, they proposed that I request to see my children. I answered that I had nothing to request, and that if I asked for something, it would be to go to confession, but that since I was refused this, I would ask for nothing. They contacted my children to have them request to see me. It was not difficult for them to obtain what one wanted to offer them before they might have even asked for it. They came. And I lost the sweetness of my life from that moment by the torments that they caused me. As soon as the oldest had arrived, they began to quarrel ceaselessly in front of me and made me suffer a lot.

I had neither the idea nor the desire to leave prison. I had imagined myself staying there for the rest of my life. The thought of staying alone there made me very happy. I felt myself become weaker every day, and I waited for the end of my life with delight.

Monsieur de Paris would have had great remorse for letting me die in prison, he admitted to his friends. I have learned this since from a very reliable source. He said once that there was only hearsay, and that he had not known any evil in me. Monsieur de Saint-Sulpice incited him against me by trying to take away his scruples so much that he could not sleep from it.

He had my children told to ask for my freedom, and he pushed the process forward as they did it, for there were reasons why he could not make the request himself. It is easy to understand that a man of this standing and of this character does not change his mind easily when things have been pushed to certain extremes. And as for me, I got this justice because his reputation being more necessary to the Church than mine, he was not obligated to destroy himself. He could merely say that he had been surprised by the appearance of things that had been attributed to me, but that, having gotten to the bottom of it and not having found them true, it was necessary to give me my freedom.

It is certain that they were letting me go unconditionally to my son's home when my release was granted. From the moment he arrived, he told me that he would only receive me on the condition that he wanted them to ask this of him in writing. He made them do as he wanted, with an extreme rigor. His very bizarre conduct made me resolve to stay where I was, and I said that I did not want to leave. Monsieur de Saint-Mars, who found this procedure odious, offered me another apartment where I would see whomever I pleased. Father Martineau advised me to leave; Monsieur Huguet and the others as well. They told me that I would always be underfoot, subject to their whims, implicating me in new things. But what made me determined more than the rest was the belief that, my conduct justifying me in the future, my friends would also be justified by the kindness they have shown me, because, as my dear Master said to his disciples: "I sanctify myself for them" (John 17:19). For my principal reason for writing this—when death might appear at any instant to end my destiny, and with my no longer claiming anything on earth except you, O my Lord, and you alone—has been the glory of God, and that contemplative prayer might not be harmed by accusing those who sincerely practice it of crimes.

Whatever aversions I might have had about going to my son's home, I let go of them due to the entreaties that were being made to me. But although before my release from the Bastille he had displayed some behavior that made me fear exposure to his boiling and violent moods, I swear that I never imagined I would receive the treatment that I suffered for the whole time that I lived with him. God, who had always led me by the cross, permitted me to find one of them there with a very particular nature. I was, however, going above and beyond to do everything possible to please him and his wife: little presents, friendly gestures, precautions of all sorts. But nothing could win them over. You alone know, O my God, the nature of the sufferings of all sorts that I endured in the course of the three or four years that I lived there.

My presence coming to bother them a lot for reasons about which I will remain silent, they wrote a letter to M. de Pontchartrain[1] that might have caused me to be put back in the Bastille if not for the fact that, to inform himself of the truth of the facts that the letter contained, this minister sent for Monsieur the Bishop of Blois.[2] This prelate was informed not only about the violent behavior of my son and the bad treatment that I suffered continually, for he took no care in hiding it, but also of the motives that had prompted him to a process of this nature, of which few examples would be found. Monsieur de Blois wrote to the Court in a very honest manner about my situation, changed the impressions that such a letter had caused and proposed of his own accord to have me change residences. The order was drawn up for M. de Pontchartrain to do this, and he was very willing to take the trouble to come to my son's home to plan the execution of it. Although my son was very comfortable with the basis of this separation, the way in which it was handled displeased him, and he had Monsieur de Blois understand that, having been charged with my supervision upon my release from the Bastille, he felt himself obligated to bring me back there or to go there himself and show a letter that he said was from Monsieur d'Argenson, who had put him in charge of me. Whatever insistence M. de Blois might have communicated to him to obey the order that he had sent, never did he want to submit to it. Monsieur de B[lois] promised me that he would write once again to Monsieur de P[ontchartrain] to remove this unforeseen difficulty.

Indeed, a few days later, he received a new order for my son to let me go to a house that I had rented in conjunction with the prelate, in a little town about half a league³ from his home, until further orders. Monsieur de Blois kept the *lettre de cachet* in which he had me write that he had transmitted me, and that I would obey him with respect. This prelate showed me a lot of goodness at this time, and I told him of the rest that I had tasted in this solitude. However, since my life was consecrated to the cross, as soon as the spirit started to breathe after so many setbacks, the body found itself overcome by all sorts of infirmities. And I had almost continuous illnesses that often put me at death's door, the air being extremely contrary to me.

I stayed there for three years this way, but with the owner no longer wanting me to continue the lease, Monsieur de Blois made an agreement that I would live in the town where I am presently, and where I do not doubt that my dear Master will save up fiercer and stronger, though less dazzling, crosses for me, until the end of my days.

Notes

INTRODUCTION

1. Patricia Ward, *Experimental Theology in America: Madame Guyon, Fénelon, and Their Readers* (Waco, Texas: Baylor University Press, 2009), 16.

2. Jeanne-Marie Guyon, *La Vie par elle-même et autres écrits biographiques.* Édition critique avec introduction et notes par Dominique Tronc. Étude littéraire par Andrée Villard. Sources classiques, vol. 29 (Paris: Honoré Champion, 2001).

3. Michel de Certeau, *The Mystic Fable, Vol. 1: The Sixteenth and Seventeenth Centuries,* trans. Michael B. Smith (Chicago: University of Chicago Press, 1992), 101.

4. Guyon, *Short and Easy Method,* 23.6. Unless otherwise noted, abbreviated citations of all of Guyon's writings except the *Prison Narratives* and her correspondence refer to the translations in *Jeanne Guyon: Selected Writings,* trans. and ed. Dianne Guenin-Lelle and Ronney Mourad (Mahwah, N.J.: Paulist Press, forthcoming 2012).

5. Guyon, *Life,* 3.17.10.

6. Ibid.

7. Ibid., 3.17.9.

8. Ibid., 3.14.13.

9. François Fénelon, *Pages nouvelles pour servir à l'étude des origines du quiétisme avant 1694,* publiées par Marcel Langlois (Paris: Desclée de Brouwer, 1934), 130–143; see Nicole Ferrier-Caverivière, *L'Image de Louis XIV dans la littérature française de 1660–1715* (Paris: Presses Universitaires de France, 1981), 288–305.

10. Max Gallo, *Louis XIV: L'Hiver du grand roi* (Paris: Pocket, 2007), 125–126.

11. Fénelon, *Pages nouvelles,* 130–131.

12. This according to Joseph Delort, *Histoire de la détention des philosophes et des gens de lettres,* t. III (Paris: Firmin Didot, 1829), cited in Louis Guerrier, *Madame Guyon: Sa vie, sa doctrine et son influence d'après les écrits originaux et des documents inédits* (Orléans: H. Herluison, Libraire-Éditeur, 1881), 293.

13. Guerrier, *Madame Guyon,* 284.

14. A good new translation is included in Chad Helms, *Fénelon: Selected Writings* (Mahwah, N.J.: Paulist Press, 2006).

15. Guyon, *Short and Easy Method*, 1.1.
16. Gallo, *Louis XIV*, 152.
17. Marie-Louise Gondal, Introduction to *Récits de captivité, Inédit: Autobiographie, Quatrième partie*, by Jeanne-Marie Guyon, texte établi, présenté, et annoté par Marie-Louise Gondal (Grenoble: Éditions Jérôme Millon, 1992), 20.
18. Guyon, *Prison Narratives*, Ch. 8.
19. Elissa D. Gelfand, *Imagination in Confinement: Women's Writings from French Prisons* (Ithaca: Cornell University Press, 1983), 64–65.
20. Guyon, *Prison Narratives*, Ch. 8.
21. Many of the factual claims in this section are drawn from Marie-Louise Gondal, Introduction to *Récits de captivité*, and "L'autobiographie de Madame Guyon. La découverte et l'apport de deux nouveaux manuscrits," *XVIIe siècle* 164 (1989): 307–323.
22. Gondal, Introduction to *Récits de captivité*, 17–18. Unless otherwise noted, all translations of quotations from French secondary sources are ours.
23. Ibid., 18.
24. Marjolaine Chevallier, "Madame Guyon et Pierre Poiret," in *Madame Guyon*, J. Beaude et al. (Grenoble: Jérôme Millon, 1997), 42.
25. Dominique Tronc, *Les années d'épreuves de Madame Guyon: Emprisonnements et interrogatoires sous le Roi Très Chrétien* (Paris: Honoré Champion, 2009), 149–274.
26. Ibid., 300–341.
27. Guyon, *Prison Narratives*, Ch. 5.
28. Ibid., Ch. 6.
29. Ibid., Ch. 2.
30. Guyon, *Life*, 3.10.1.
31. Ibid., 3.10.2.
32. Nicholas Paige, *Being Interior: Autobiography and the Contradictions of Modernity in Seventeenth-Century France* (Philadelphia: University of Pennsylvania Press, 2001), 172.
33. Ibid., 172–74.
34. Guyon, *Life*, 3.17.1.
35. Bossuet, *La Relation sur le quiétisme*, in *Oeuvres*, ed. Abbé Velat and Yvonne Champailler (Paris: Gallimard, 1970), 1105, quoted in Marie-Florine Bruneau, *Women Mystics Confront the Modern World: Marie de l'Incarnation (1599–1672) and Madame Guyon (1648–1717)* (Albany: SUNY, 1998), 192. The translation is Bruneau's. Bossuet refers here to Guyon, *Life*, 3.1.9.
36. Guyon, *Life*, 3.21.1.
37. See, for example, Jeanne Guyon, *Madame Guyon et Fénelon: La Correspondance secrète, avec un choix de poésies spirituelles*, édition préparée par Benjamin Perrot (Paris: Dervy-Livres, 1982), Letter 127. Subsequent references to this text will be cited as *Correspondance*.

38. Guyon, *Short and Easy Method,* Ch. 22.

39. Guyon, *Life,* 3.14.10.

40. Guyon, *Prison Narratives,* Ch. 5.

41. Rémy Saisselin, *The Rule of Reason and the Ruses of the Heart: A Philosophical Dictionary of Classical French Criticism, Critics, and Aesthetic Issues* (Cleveland: Case Western Reserve University, 1970), 47–48.

42. Guyon, *Prison Narratives,* Ch. 4.

43. Ibid.

44. Ibid., Ch. 5.

45. Ibid., Ch. 4.

46. Ibid., Ch. 5.

47. See Mallet-Joris's historical overview of attitudes surrounding Guyon (Françoise Mallet-Joris, *Jeanne Guyon* [Paris: Flammarion, 1978]) as well as the more recent treatment in Russo's description of the relationship of Fénelon and Guyon (Elena Russo, *Styles of Enlightenment: Taste, Politics, and Authorship in Eighteenth-Century France* [Baltimore: The Johns Hopkins University Press, 2007], 87).

48. Ferrier-Caverivière, *L'Image de Louis XIV,* 238.

49. Guerrier, *Madame Guyon,* 302.

50. Joanna Summers, *Late-Medieval Prison Writing and the Politics of Autobiography* (New York: Oxford University Press, 2004), 21.

51. W. Clark Gilpin, "The Letter from Prison in Christian History and Theology," *Religion and Culture Web Forum,* The Martin Marty Center for the Advanced Study of Religion, January 2003. Gilpin's essay concerns English prison letters of the sixteenth and seventeenth centuries, and some of what he writes is specific to that context. His comments nonetheless suggest many useful parallels to Guyon's (non-epistolary, French) narrative, especially given that many of the authors he analyzes were imprisoned for religious non-conformity.

52. Arlette Lebrige, "Justice et raison d'état. Les vicissitudes d'une enquête," in Dominique Tronc, *Les années d'épreuves de Madame Guyon,* 31–35.

53. Ioan Davies, *Writers in Prison* (Oxford: Basil Blackwell, 1990), 16.

54. Ibid., 18.

55. Guyon, *Life,* 3.14.13.

56. Guyon, *Prison Narratives,* Ch. 1.

57. Ibid.

58. Ibid.

59. Ibid., Ch. 3.

60. Ibid., Ch. 6.

61. Ibid., Ch. 3.

62. Ibid., Ch. 6.

63. Gilpin, "The Letter from Prison."

64. One letter from François La Combe and Sieur de Lasherous contains the salutation, "The little Church [*petite Église*] sends you greetings, illustrious persecuted

one" and another refers to her supporters as "the children of the Little Master" (*les enfants du Petit Maître*). These expressions raised the concern that Guyon was leading a sectarian movement.

65. Gilpin, "The Letter from Prison."
66. Ibid.
67. Guyon, *Prison Narratives*, Ch. 7.
68. Guyon, *Life*, 3.7.8.
69. Guyon, *Correspondance*, Letter 71.
70. Guyon, *Prison Narratives*, Preface.
71. Gilpin, "The Letter from Prison."
72. Ibid.
73. Guyon, *Prison Narratives*, Ch. 7.
74. Ibid., Ch. 1.
75. Guyon, *Life*, 3.20.1.
76. Ibid., 3.20.4.
77. Gondal, Introduction to *Récits de captivité*, 19.
78. Dominique Tronc, Introduction to Jeanne-Marie Guyon, *La Vie par elle-même et autres écrits biographiques*, 99.
79. Chevallier, "Madame Guyon et Pierre Poiret," 46.
80. Ward, *Experimental Theology in America*, 16.
81. Guyon, *Prison Narratives*, Ch. 8.
82. Ibid..
83. W. R. Ward, *Early Evangelicalism: A Global Intellectual History, 1670–1789* (Cambridge: Cambridge University Press, 2006), 61–69.
84. Guyon, *Life*, 3.21.4.
85. "O my God, let everything fall on me, let me be the scapegoat to atone for the faults of your people, but spare the good and do not permit your saints to become food for the birds of the air and the beasts of the earth."
86. Dreams play an interesting role throughout this text and in Guyon's autobiography as a whole. As is consistent with early modern discourse about their religious significance, Guyon usually interprets her dreams as forms of spiritual communication. Sometimes she presents them as predictive of the future. At other times they reveal deep truths in symbolic forms.
87. Guyon, *Prison Narratives*, Ch. 1.
88. Ibid.
89. Ibid., Ch. 2.
90. Ibid.
91. Ibid., Ch. 7.
92. Ibid., Ch. 6.
93. Ibid., Ch. 1.
94. Ibid., Ch. 8.
95. Ibid., Ch. 2.

96. Jeanne Guyon, *Short and Easy Method*, 7.1–3.

97. Davies, *Writers in Prison*, 22.

98. Gilpin, "The Letter from Prison."

99. Guyon, *Short and Easy Method,* Ch. 7.

100. Guyon, *Correspondance*, Letter 96.

101. Gelfand, *Imagination in Confinement*, 15.

102. Ibid., 29.

103. Ibid., 113.

104. Ibid., 21.

105. Ibid., 121.

106. Ibid., 42.

107. Guyon, *Prison Narratives*, Ch. 5.

108. Ibid., Ch. 2.

109. Gelfand, *Imagination in Confinement*, 43.

110. Guyon, *Prison Narratives*, Ch. 4.

111. Ibid.

112. Ibid., Ch. 1.

113. Guyon, *Life*, 3.10.

114. Gelfand, *Imagination in Confinement*, 113.

115. Guyon, *Prison Narratives*, Ch. 7.

116. Gelfand, *Imagination in Confinement*, 124.

117. Ibid., 128.

118. Ibid., 42.

119. Ibid., 111.

120. Louis Cognet, *Post-Reformation Spirituality,* trans. P. Hepburne Scott (New York: Hawthorne Books, 1959), 136.

121. Ward, *Experimental Theology in America*.

122. For more reflections on the play of 'silence' and 'silencing' in female discourse, see Lynn Theismeyer's *Discourse and Silencing: Representation and the Language of Displacement*. (Amsterdam and Philadelphia: John Benjamins Publishing Company, 2003).

123. Quoted in Mallet-Joris, *Jeanne Guyon,* 489.

124. L.-A. Bonnel, *Sur la Controverse de Bossuet et de Fénelon sur le Quiétisme* (Macon: Imprimerie de Dejussieu, 1850), xl-xli.

125. Some examples of these references in recent scholarship include Elena Russo, *Styles of Enlightenment: Taste, Politics, and Authorship in Eighteenth-Century France* (Baltimore: The Johns Hopkins University Press, 2007), 87; Robin Briggs, *Communities of Belief: Cultural and Social Tensions in Early Modern France* (Oxford: Clarendon, 1989), 224–225; and Janet Gurkin Altman, "Women's Letters in the Public Sphere," in Elizabeth C. Goldsmith and Dena Goodman, *Women's Letters* (Ithaca and London: Cornell University Press, 1995), 109.

126. Gallo, *Louis XIV*, 83.

127. Ibid., 125.

128. Ibid., 129.

129. Ibid., 141.

130. See Ward, *Experimental Theology in America*, for an historical analysis of the generally positive and sometimes even reverent reception of Guyon's work outside France.

131. Thomas Cogwell Upham, *Life and Religious Opinions and Experience of Madame de La Mothe Guyon* (New York: Harper and Brothers, 1849).

132. Ronald Knox, *Enthusiasm: A Chapter in the History of Religion with Special Reference to the Seventeenth and Eighteenth Centuries* (New York: Oxford University Press, 1961), 235.

133. While devotional interest in Guyon has been most common among English-speaking Protestants, recent scholarly interest in her has been strong among French authors, most of whom situate Guyon more accurately in her historical and spiritual milieu than the editors of the Protestant presses who continue to sell translations of her books. Although, as discussed above, a few of these authors continue to present her uncharitably, some of the best recent scholarship about Guyon has come from historians such as Jacques Le Brun and Jean-Robert Armogathe whose investigations have been partly motivated by Catholic theological interests.

CHAPTER 1

1. In Jeanne Guyon, *The Life of Madame J.M.B. de la Mothe Guyon Written by Herself,* 3.20.1 and 3.20.4, subsequently referred to as *"Life."*

2. Jacques-Bénigne Bossuet, the Bishop of Meaux.

3. Tronc states that this is a reference to Gilles Fouquet, who was the uncle of Guyon's son-in-law Louis-Nicolas Fouquet, son of Nicolas Fouquet, the disgraced finance minister under Louis XIV (Jeanne-Marie Guyon, *La Vie par elle-même et autres écrits biographiques.* Édition critique avec introduction et notes par Dominique Tronc. Étude littéraire par Andrée Villard. Sources classiques, vol. 29 [Paris: Champion, 2001], 883). All subsequent references to this critical edition of the *Life* will be cited as "Tronc."

4. François Desgrez, a police lieutenant.

5. Gabriel Nicolas de La Reynie, Lieutenant General of Police in Paris.

6. François La Combe, the Barnabite Friar who had a strong influence on Guyon's religious development and eventually became her spiritual director.

7. These letters have been reprinted in Dominique Tronc, *Les Années d'épreuves de Madame Guyon: Emprisonnements et interrogatoires sous le Roi Très Chrétien* (Paris: Honoré Champion, 2009), 116–21.

8. Jansenism was a Catholic theological movement especially associated with the schools created at the convent of Port-Royal-des-Champs near Paris in 1637. Its

opponents compared it to Calvinism because of its emphasis on the unmerited and irresistible character of divine grace, the complete depravity of fallen human nature, and God's predestination of the elect for salvation. The Jansenists claimed support for their views in Augustine's writings on human freedom and divine grace. After Pope Urban VIII condemned the movement's foundational text, *Augustinus* by Cornelius Otto Jansen, in 1642, Jansenism in France became increasingly embattled. By Guyon's time, Jansenism was an officially condemned but still powerful underground movement, which retained the sympathies of many prominent theologians and clerics. Many Jansenists, most famously Pierre Nicole, were prominent critics of Quietism.

9. Grislidy (most often spelled Griselda in English) is a virtuous, long-suffering heroine in the *Decameron*; Boccaccio is presumed to have based her story on several earlier narratives in which the character appears, dating back to the eleventh century.

10. The next two paragraphs are repeated here, almost identically, from the *Life*, 3.20.

11. Guyon considers it unfaithful to "premeditate" her response to her interrogators because, in doing so, she reasons for herself instead of simply submitting to God's activity in her. She claims that the fullest union with God requires a complete annihilation of the self, including its reason, memory, and will. When she allows her own will and reason to be fully submitted to God, she finds that God, speaking through her, supplies perfect responses to her interrogators. Consider the following episode from her *Life* in which she defends her writing against criticisms from Bossuet, the Bishop of Meaux: "There is little imagination in what I write because I often write what I have never thought. What I would have wished for M. de Meaux was that he not judge me by reason but by his heart. I had not premeditated any response before seeing him; the plain truth alone was all my strength, and I found myself content that my mistake would be known as the grace of God. My wretchedness might be mixed with his pure light, but can mud tarnish the sun?" (*Life*, 3.14.4)

12. Inspired by Luke 21:14–15 (Tronc).

13. Father Léonard Pirot, a theologian at the Sorbonne, whose interrogation of Guyon is reported in the *Life*, 3.5.

14. Monsieur Charon, an official working for François de Harlay de Champvallon, the previous Archbishop of Paris. Guyon discusses his role in her first confinement in Paris in her *Life*, 3.1–3.7.

15. An allusion to Jesus' remark to Nicodemus, John 3:10 (Tronc).

16. This is probably "the Good Franciscan" who introduced Guyon to Geneviève Granger years before. See Tronc, 194.

17. Joachim Trotti de La Chétardie, according to Gondal (Jeanne-Marie Guyon, *Récits de captivité*, Texte établi, présenté, et annoté par Marie-Louise Gondal [Grenoble: Éditions Jérôme Millon, 1992], 46). All subsequent references to this edition will be cited as "Gondal."

18. Louis Tronson, the Superior at Saint-Sulpice and one of Guyon's official examiners at the Issy Conference, a series of hearings about disputed mystical claims that included formal investigations of Guyon's writings.

19. Louis-Antoine de Noailles, Archbishop of Paris, led Guyon's persecution at this stage.

CHAPTER 2

1. The man in charge of the prison at Vincennes (Tronc, 901).
2. A weekly publication of news and works of literature.
3. François de Salignac de la Mothe-Fénelon (1651–1715), Archbishop of Cambrai, Guyon's friend, confidant, and defender, and a celebrated mystic.
4. See *Life*, 3.19.7–8.
5. The preceding paragraph is repeated in *Life*, 3.20.7.
6. Although Guyon recognizes that experiences of prophetic foreknowledge can be dangerous and lead to self-deception (see *Life*, 1.9.7), she also claims to have received this spiritual gift in several of her writings. For example, she claims foreknowledge of La Combe's future spiritual state (*Life*, 2.22.8) and of Fénelon's (*Correspondance*, Letter 38). She claims to have seen Fénelon in a dream eight years before she actually met him (*Life*, 3.10.1). Guyon also claims to have received other miraculous spiritual gifts such as the powers of exorcism, healing, and spiritual communication (*Life*, 2.12). She defends herself here against the accusation, in Chapter 4, that her inaccurate prophecy about the King proves that her spiritual claims are delusional. Later, in Chapter 6, she reports her true prediction that her prison guard would not become governor of the Bastille as he hoped.
7. "Je fis le Carême à feu et à sang."
8. A woman who made false accusations about Guyon when she was teaching at St-Cyr.
9. A priest who was burned at the stake in 1611 (Tronc, 911).
10. Fénelon, according to Gondal, 76, n. 31.

CHAPTER 3

1. First a royal palace, then a medieval prison, the place of Marie-Antoinette's imprisonment before being guillotined during the Revolution.
2. The Parliament of Paris in the seventeenth century was primarily a court of appeal rather than a parliament in the contemporary sense, although it also had limited legislative authority and recorded and enacted royal edicts. It heard both civil and criminal cases. Positions on the court were filled by nobles and were either inherited or purchased from the King. Although the Parliament was heavily influenced by the King, it had some independent power and applied fairly consistent rules of

evidence in judicial proceedings (although these included the routine use of torture to exact confessions).

3. This refers to "the affair concerning the *Maxims of the Saints* [written by Fénelon]. Bossuet's *Account of Quietism* had been distributed on June 26 and had made quite a stir. Confronted with Fénelon's resistance to oral retractions, and under pressure from Bossuet, Louis XIV wrote to the Pope on July 26 to ask him to make a pronouncement. On August 3, Fénelon was exiled from the Court" (Gondal, 81, n. 2).

4. The ecu was a large silver coin. Its value fluctuated throughout the seventeenth century, but it was probably worth at least three francs at this time. Guyon was therefore charged considerably more than the original quoted price.

5. Uncertain of term (Tronc).

6. One of Guyon's maids, mentioned above in Chapter 1.

7. Tronc explains that this refers to *The Life of Jean d'Arenthon d'Alex, Bishop and Prince of Geneva* by Dom Innocent Le Masson (Tronc, 925).

8. *Life*, 2.3.

9. Superior at the Visitation Sainte-Marie convent in Paris.

CHAPTER 4

1. After Deut. 18:22.

2. "Women should be silent in the churches. For they are not permitted to speak, but should be subordinate, as the law also says" (1 Cor. 14:34, NRSV). "Let a woman learn in silence with full submission. I permit no woman to teach or to have authority over a man; she is to keep silent" (1 Tim. 2:11–12, NRSV).

3. The allusion here is probably to the *Journal des Savants* (Tronc, 933).

4. A type of finch.

CHAPTER 5

1. An invitation to put the shirt on the King during the ritual of dressing him, a sign of high privilege.

2. A sealed letter containing direct and irrefutable orders from the King, often concerning arrest or imprisonment.

3. A medicine similar to quinine produced from tree bark.

CHAPTER 6

1. June 4, 1698 (Tronc).

2. A guard at the Bastille.

3. This probably refers to *Emblems of Divine Love* (*Emblèmes de l'amour divin*), by Otto Vaenius. Guyon wrote several spiritual poems inspired by the images in this book.

4. Marc-René de Voyer de Paulmy d'Argenson, the man who replaced La Reynie as Lieutenant General of Police in Paris.

5. The governor of the Bastille, Monsieur de St-Mars.

6. "trouvé la pie au nid"—literally, "found the magpie in the nest."

7. The remainder of this paragraph is copied almost exactly from *Life*, 3.20.7.

8. A reference to Pope Innocent XII having condemned Fénelon for his *Maxims of the Saints* in 1699.

CHAPTER 7

1. In Chapter 3.

2. The remainder of this paragraph was inserted by a copyist (Tronc, 965, n. 105).

3. "O happy fault." This phrase is part of the "Exultet," intoned during the Easter Vigil.

4. After Ps. 66:12. In Gondal's edition there are two more paragraphs here, which seem to have been added by a later copyist. Tronc has moved them to an earlier passage in 4.7, and we follow Tronc's edition here.

5. Tronc suggests that this is a reference to Mme de Bernaville, the wife of the commander of the Bastille (Tronc, 975).

CHAPTER 8

1. Louis II Phélypeaux, Count of Pontchartrain, who was secretary of state under Louis XIV.

2. Monsignor David-Nicolas de Bertier.

3. About two kilometers.

Bibliography

Aegerter, Emmanuel. 1941. *Madame Guyon: Une aventurière mystique*. Paris: Librairie Hachette.

Armogathe, Jean-Robert. 1973. *Le Quiétisme*. Paris: Presses Universitaires de France.

Armstrong, Regis J., and Ignatius C. Brady, Eds. 1988. *Francis De Sales, Jane De Chantal: Letters of Spiritual Direction*. Mahwah, N.J.: Paulist Press.

Balsama, George. 1973. "Madame Guyon, Heterodox…" *Church History* 42: 350–365.

Bayley, Peter. 1999. "What was Quietism Subversive Of?" *Seventeenth-Century French Studies* 21: 195–204.

Beasley, Faith. 2000. "Altering the Fabric of History: Women's Participation in the Classical Age," in *A History of Women's Writing*. Edited by Sonya Stephens. Cambridge: Cambridge University Press.

Beaude, J., et al. 1997. *Madame Guyon: Rencontre autour de la vie et l'œuvre de Madame Guyon*. Grenoble: Jérôme Millon.

Bertrand, Dominique. 1995. *Dire le rire à l'âge classique: Représenter pour mieux contrôler*. Aix-en-Provence: Publications de l'Université de Provence.

Bossuet, Jacques Bénigne. 1970. *La Relation sur le quiétisme*, in *Oeuvres*. Edited by Abbé Velat and Yvonne Champailler. Paris: Gallimard, 1970.

Bremond, Henri. 1910. *Apologie pour Fénelon*. Paris: Perrin.

Briggs, Robin. 1995. *Communities of Belief: Cultural and Social Tensions in Early Modern France*. Oxford: Clarendon.

Broekhuysen, Arthus. 1991. "The Quietist Movement and Miguel de Molinos." *The Journal of Religion and Psychical Research* 14: 139–143.

Brombert, Victor. 1978. *The Romantic Prison: The French Tradition*. Princeton: Princeton University Press.

Bruneau, Marie-Florine. 1998. *Women Mystics Confront the Modern World: Marie de l'Incarnation (1599–1672) and Madame Guyon (1648–1717)*. SUNY Series in Western Esoteric Traditions. Albany, N.Y.: State University of New York Press.

Bruno, Jean. 1962. "L'Expérience mystique de Madame Guyon." Introduction to *La Vie de Madame Guyon écrite par elle-même* in *Les Cahiers de la Tour St-Jacques VI*. Paris: Roudil.

Chang, Leah L. 2009. *Into Print: The Production of Female Authorship in Early Modern France*. Newark: University of Delaware Press.

Chevallier, Marjolaine. 1997. "Madame Guyon et Pierre Poiret," in *Madame Guyon: Rencontre autour de la vie et l'œuvre de Madame Guyon*, by J. Beaude et al. Grenoble: Jérôme Millon.

Cholakin, Patricia. 2000. *Women and the Politics of Self-Representation in Seventeenth-Century France*. Newark: University of Delaware Press.

Cognet, Louis. 1959. *Post-Reformation Spirituality*. Translated by P. Hepburne Scott. New York: Hawthorne Books.

———. 1981. "Ecclesiastical Life in France," in *History of the Church 6: The Church in the Age of Absolutism and Enlightenment*. Edited by Hubert Jedin and John Dolan. Translated by Gunther J. Holst. New York: Crossroads.

Daly, Pierrette. 1993. *Heroic Tropes: Gender and Intertext*. Detroit: Wayne State University Press.

Davies, Ioan. 1990. *Writers in Prison*. Oxford: Basil Blackwell.

De Certeau, Michel. 1988. *The Writing of History*. Translated by Tom Conley. New York: Columbia University Press.

———. 1992. *The Mystic Fable, Vol. 1: The Sixteenth and Seventeenth Centuries*. Translated by Michael B. Smith. Chicago: University of Chicago Press.

De La Bedoyere, Michael. 1956. *The Archbishop and the Lady: The Story of Fénelon and Madame Guyon*. New York: Pantheon.

Delacroix, Henri. 1922. *La Religion et la foi*. Paris: Librairie Félix Alcan.

———. 1938. *Les Grands mystiques chrétiens*. Paris: Librairie Félix Alcan.

Delort, Joseph. *Histoire de la détention des philosophes et des gens de lettres*. Paris: Firmin Didot, 1829.

DiPiero, Thomas. 1992. *Dangerous Truths & Criminal Passions: The Evolution of the French Novel, 1569–1791*. Stanford: Stanford University Press.

DuBois, Elfrieda. 1986. "Fénelon and Quietism," in *The Study of Spirituality*. Edited by Cheslyn Jones, Geoffrey Wainwright, and Edward Yarnold, SJ. New York and Oxford: Oxford University Press.

Dumas, François Ribadeau. 1968. *Fénelon et les saintes folies de Madame Guyon*. Geneva: Éditions du Mont-Blanc.

Dupré, Louis. 1989. "Jansenism and Quietism," in *Christian Spirituality: Post-Reformation and Modern*. Edited by Louis Dupré and Don E. Saliers, in collaboration with John Meyendorff. Vol. 18 of *World Spirituality: An Encyclopedic History of the Religious Quest*. New York: Crossroads.

Fanning, Steven. 2001. *Mystics of the Christian Tradition*. New York: Routledge.

Fénelon, François. 1934. *Pages nouvelles pour servir à l'étude des origines du quiétisme avant 1694*. Published by Marcel Langlois. Paris: Desclée de Brouwer.

Ferrier-Caverivière, Nicole. 1981. *L'Image de Louis XIV dans la littérature française de 1660–1715*. Paris: Presses Universitaires de France.

Forthomme, Bernard, and Jad Hatem. 1997. *Madame Guyon: Quiétude d'accélération*. Paris: Cariscript.

France, Peter. 1992. *Politeness and Its Discontents: Problems in French Classical Culture.* Cambridge: Cambridge University Press.

Fraser, Antonia. 2007. *Love and Louis XIV: The Women in the Life of the Sun King.* New York: Anchor Books.

Gallo, Max. 2007. *Louis XIV: L'hiver du grand roi.* Paris: Pocket.

Gelfand, Elissa D. 1983. *Imagination in Confinement: Women's Writings from French Prisons.* Ithaca: Cornell University Press.

Gilpin, W. Clark. 2003. "The Letter from Prison in Christian History and Theology." *Religion and Culture Web Forum.* The Martin Marty Center for the Advanced Study of Religion. January 2003.

Goldsmith, Elizabeth C. 2001. *Publishing Women's Life Stories in France, 1647–1720: From Voice to Print.* Burlington, Vt.: Ashgate.

Goldsmith, Elizabeth C., and Dena Goodman. 1995. *Women's Letters.* Ithaca: Cornell University Press.

Gondal, Marie Louise. 1989. *Madame Guyon (1648–1717): Un nouveau visage.* Paris: Beauchesne.

———. 1989. "L'autobiographie de Madame Guyon. La découverte et l'apport de deux nouveaux manuscrits." *XVIIe siècle* 164: 307–323.

———. 1992. "Présentation." Introduction to Guyon, Jeanne-Marie Bouvier de la Mothe. *Récits de captivité, Inédit: Autobiographie, Quatrième partie.* Texte établi, présenté et annoté par Marie-Louise Gondal. Grenoble: Jérôme Millon.

———. 1998. "*Traité du purgatoire,*" suivi de "*Trois moyens de purification et de mort*" et "*Figures scripturaires de la purification.*" Grenoble: Jérôme Millon.

Goubert, Pierre. 1970. *Louis XIV and Twenty Million Frenchmen.* Translated by Anne Carter. New York: Vintage.

Grenier, Jean. 1984. *Écrits sur le quiétisme.* Quimper: Calligrammes.

Guerrier, Louis. 1881. *Madame Guyon: Sa vie, sa doctrine et son influence d'après les écrits originaux et des documents inédits.* Orléans: H. Herluison, Libraire-Éditeur.

Guiguet, Jean-Claude. 1999. "Madame Guyon à Thonon." *Étude* 3902: 237–240.

Gurkin Altman, Janet. 1995. "Women's Letters in the Public Sphere," in Elizabeth C. Goldsmith and Dena Goodman, *Women's Letters.* Ithaca and London: Cornell University Press.

Guyon, Jeanne-Marie Bouvier de la Mothe. 1982. *Jeanne Guyon, Madame Guyon et Fénelon: La Correspondance secrète, avec un choix de poésies spirituelles.* Édition préparée par Benjamin Perrot. Paris: Dervy-Livres.

———. 1992. *Récits de captivité, Inédit: Autobiographie, Quatrième partie.* Texte établi, présenté et annoté par Marie-Louise Gondal. Grenoble: Jérôme Millon.

———. 2001. *La Vie par elle-même, et autres écrits biographiques.* Édition critique avec introduction et notes par Dominique Tronc. Étude littéraire par Andrée Villard. Sources classiques, vol. 29. Paris: Honoré Champion.

———. Forthcoming 2012. *Jeanne Guyon: Selected Writings.* Translated, edited, and introduced by Dianne Guenin-Lelle and Ronney Mourad. Mahwah, N.J.: Paulist Press.

Harth, Erica. 1983. *Ideology and Culture in Seventeenth-Century France.* Ithaca: Cornell University Press.

Helms, Chad. 2006. *Fénelon: Selected Writings.* Mahwah, N.J.: Paulist Press.

Heuberger, Jean Marc. 2001. "Les commentaires bibliques de Madame Guyon dans la Bible de Berleburg." *Revue de théologie et de philosophie* 133: 303–323.

James, Nancy. 2007. *The Pure Love of Jeanne Guyon: The Great Conflict in King Louis XIV's Court.* Lanham, Md.: University Press of America.

Jantzen, Grace. 1996. *Power, Gender and Christian Mysticism.* New York: Cambridge University Press.

Knox, Ronald. 1961. *Enthusiasm: A Chapter in the History of Religion with Special Reference to the Seventeenth and Eighteenth Centuries.* New York: Oxford University Press.

Kristeva, Julia. 1987. *Tales of Love.* Translated by Leon S. Roudiez. New York: Columbia University Press.

Laude, Patrick D. 1991. *Approches du quiétisme: Deux études suivies du Moyen court et très facile pour l'oraison de Madame Guyon (texte de l'édition de 1685).* Papers on Seventeenth-Century French Literature, 57–95. Paris, Seattle, and Tübingen.

Le Brun, Jacques. 1986. "Quiétisme." *Dictionnaire de spiritualité ascétique et mystique.* Vol. 12: 2756–2842.

———. 2001. "Présupposés théoriques de la lecture mystique de la Bible: L'exemple de La Sainte Bible de Mme Guyon." *Revue de théologie et de philosophie* 133: 287–302.

Lebrige, Arlette. 2009. "Justice et raison d'état. Les vicissitudes d'une enquête," in Dominique Tronc, *Les années d'épreuves de Madame Guyon: Emprisonnements et interrogatoires sous le Roi Très Chrétien.* Paris: Honoré Champion.

Leduc-Fayette, Denise, Ed. 1996. *Fénelon, philosophie et spiritualité: Actes du colloque.* Paris: Droz.

Lindberg, Carter, Ed. 2005. *The Pietist Theologians: An Introduction to Theology in the Seventeenth and Eighteenth Centuries.* Oxford: Basil Blackwell.

Loskoutoff, Yvan. 2003. "Les Récits de songe de Jeanne Guyon à Fénelon (avec des textes inédits)" in *Songes et Songeurs (XIIIe-XVIIIe siècles).* Edited by Nathalie Dauvois and Jean-Philippe Grosperrin. Québec: Les Presses de l'Université Laval.

Mallet-Joris, Françoise. 1978. *Jeanne Guyon.* Paris: Flammarion.

Millot, Catherine. 2006. *La Vie parfaite: Jeanne Guyon, Simone Weil, Etty Hillesum.* Paris: Gallimard.

Orcibal, Jean. 1997. *Études d'histoire et de littérature religieuses XVIe-XVIIIe siècles.* Edited by Jacques Le Brun and Jean Lesalnier. Paris: Klincksieck.

Paige, Nicholas D. 2001. *Being Interior: Autobiography and the Contradictions of Modernity in Seventeenth-Century France.* Philadelphia: University of Pennsylvania Press.

Pope, Russell. 1938. "French Quietism: Jeanne Marie Guyon," in *Concerning Mysticism: Being Those Lectures Delivered at Guilford College Library in the Spring of 1938.* Guilford College Bulletin, 21.11: 13–28.

Popkin, Richard. 1992. "Fideism, Quietism, and Unbelief: Skepticism for and against Religion in the Seventeenth and Eighteenth Centuries," in *Faith, Reason, and Skepticism.* Edited with an introduction by Marcus Hester. Philadelphia: Temple University Press.

Randall, Catherine. 2000. "'Loosening the Stays:' Madame Guyon's Quietist Opposition to Absolutism." *Mystics Quarterly* 26: 8–30.

Riley, Patrick. 2002. "Blaise Pascal, Jeanne Guyon, and the Paradoxes of the *moi haïssable.*" *Papers on Seventeenth-Century French Literature* 29: 222–240.

Riley, Philip F. 2001. *A Lust for Virtue: Louis XIV's Attack on Sin in Seventeenth-Century France*. Westport, Conn.: Greenwood Press.

Rivière, Marc Serge. 1991. "The Reactions of the Anti-Voltaire Lobby to *Le Siècle de Louis XIV*: Guyon, Nonnette, Berthier and Fréron." *Studies on Voltaire & the Eighteenth Century* 292: 217–242.

Russo, Elena. 2007. *Styles of Enlightenment: Taste, Politics, and Authorship in Eighteenth-Century France*. Baltimore: The Johns Hopkins University Press.

Saisselin, Rémy. 1970. *The Rule of Reason and the Ruses of the Heart: A Philosophical Dictionary of Classical French Criticism, Critics, and Aesthetic Issues*. Cleveland: Case Western Reserve University.

Sluhovsky, Moshe. 2007. *Believe Not Every Spirit: Possession, Mysticism, & Discernment in Early Modern Catholicism*. Chicago: University of Chicago Press.

St. Ville, Susan Monica. 1996. "A Chaos without Confusion: A Study of the Mystical Discourse of Jeanne Guyon." Ph.D. dissertation, University of Chicago.

Summers, Joanna. 2004. *Late-Medieval Prison Writing and the Politics of Autobiography*. New York: Oxford University Press.

Thiesmeyer, Lynn, Ed. 2003. *Discourse and Silencing: Representation and the Language of Displacement*. Amsterdam: John Benjamins Publishing Company.

Thompson, Phyllis. 1986. *Madame Guyon, Martyr of the Holy Spirit*. London: Hodder and Stoughton.

Thompson, William M., Ed. 1989. *Bérulle and the French School*. Translated by Lowell M. Glendon. Mahwah, N.J.: Paulist Press.

Treasure, Geoffrey. 2001. *Louis XIV*. London: Pearson.

Tronc, Dominique. 2001. Introduction to *La Vie par elle-même, et autres écrits biographiques*, by Jeanne Guyon. Édition critique avec introduction et notes par Dominique Tronc. Étude littéraire par Andrée Villard. Sources classiques, vol. 29. Paris: Honoré Champion.

———. 2009. *Les années d'épreuves de Madame Guyon: Emprisonnements et interrogatoires sous le Roi Très Chrétien*. Paris: Honoré Champion.

Tyson, John R. 1999. *Invitation to Christian Spirituality: An Ecumenical Anthology*. New York and Oxford: Oxford University Press.

Upham, Thomas Cogwell. 1849. *Life and Religious Opinions and Experience of Madame de La Mothe Guyon*. New York: Harper and Brothers.

Wainwright, Geoffrey. 1976. "Revolution and Quietism: Two Political Attitudes in Theological Perspective." *Scottish Journal of Theology* 29: 535–555.

Ward, Patricia. 1995. "Madame Guyon in America: An Annotated Bibliography." *Bulletin of Bibliography* 52: 107–112.

———. 1997. "Le Quiétisme aux États-Unis," in *Madame Guyon: Rencontre autour de la vie et l'œuvre de Madame Guyon*, by J. Beaude et al. Grenoble: Jérôme Millon.

———. 1998. "Madame Guyon and Experiential Theology in America." *The American Society of Church History* 67: 484–498.

———. 2009. *Experimental Theology in America: Madame Guyon, Fénelon, and Their Readers*. Waco: Baylor University Press.

Ward, W. R. 2006. *Early Evangelicalism: A Global Intellectual History, 1670–1789*. Cambridge: Cambridge University Press.

Winn, Colette, and Donna Kuizenga, Eds. 1997. *Women Writers in Pre-Revolutionary France: Strategies of Emancipation*. New York: Garland.

Index